AF481995

"With *Winds of Change,* Dick Nasca has creatively written a wonderful novel about his Sicilian ancestors and their lives in America, which can be shared for generations to come."

— *Ed Hearn*

"Your finished product is a beneficial, straightforward and magnanimous contribution to your family history."

— *W. Jack Bostrom*

WINDS OF CHANGE

Two Sicilian Families Immigrate to America

WINDS OF CHANGE

Two Sicilian Families Immigrate to America

By Richard J. Nasca, M.D.

Published by IngramSpark

RICHARD J. NASCA

Copyright © 2023 Richard J. Nasca

All rights reserved. No part of this book may be reproduced, stored, transmitted or copied in any form, electronically or mechanically including photocopying or transmitting by any information and retrieval system, except by permission of the author.

Author's contact rjnasca@gmail.com
Published by IngramSpark
Printed by IngramSpark
Printed in USA

Disclaimer: The book is based on several sources of information which may or may not be accurate or correct. No errors, oversights, or harms were intended for any individual, organization, or company.

Dedication

It is with great respect that this book is dedicated
to all our courageous ancestors
who wanted a better life for their families.

Contents

Prologue

Winds of Change chronicles the lives of my Sicilian grandparents and their journeys to America.

Nicolo "Nick" Disparti, my maternal grandfather from Lercara Friddi, Sicily, survived a sulfur mine explosion as a youth, a ship fire on his voyage to America and a salt mine explosion in western New York. Coworkers at the salt mine discovered him unconscious after a gas explosion and he was fired. He found work as a small-town laborer, bought a home, had five children with his wife, Fortunata Latona Disparti, and managed to raise several varieties of grapes, which were in great demand by local wineries.

Giuseppe "Joseph" Nasca, my paternal grandfather from Cerda, Sicily, who had never worked in a mine, was contracted to work in the coal mines in Pittston, Pennsylvania at age thirty-three for his passage to America. He sold bananas out of a pushcart, and his wife, Maria Epifania, managed a boarding house for miners until they saved enough money to purchase a grocery store in Rochester, New York, to serve the needs of the local immigrants. Joseph and Maria had six children. The young family continued to thrive despite the Great Depression, his supply trucks being robbed by Mafia gangs and his store being marked with the sign of the "Black Hand" of the Mafia.

Nothing you read in Winds of Change should be taken

as verifiable. However, I believe that the majority of what you are about to read did occur and every major character did exist. Parts of this book are based on conjecture, educated supposition, and at times guesswork which may not be historically accurate. A great deal of the content was sourced from oral accounts provided by my parents, Lena and Joseph Nasca, and by siblings, cousins and other relatives. Further information was obtained through Ancestry. com, newspapers, family correspondence and photographs.

Part I

CHAPTER 1

The Disparti Family

Generations of the Disparti family had lived in the same stone house since 1729, in the town of Lercara Friddi, Sicily, about forty-five kilometers from Palermo, the capital city. There were many small towns in the region surrounded by verdant fields of vegetable farms and vineyards. Lercara Friddi, "Little Palermo," was known for its production of fava beans, artichokes, grapes and sulfur. Frank Sinatra's parents were from Lercara Friddi. Mafia boss "Lucky" Luciano (Salvatore Luciana) was born there in 1896.

Sulfur has been mined in Sicily since 900 BC. There was a large mine near Lercara Friddi that infused a great deal of additional revenue into the local community. Most of the ore was exported to Greece and North Africa to produce agricultural chemicals. The majority of sulfur used in different parts of the world came from Sicily.

The town had a large Catholic Church, Santa Maria Della Neve; many shops; local and government offices; and several streets of small stone and stucco homes perched along narrow, hilly streets connected to the center of town.

Girolamo Disparti and Vincenza Sangiorgio, my maternal great-grandparents, were married in 1866. Girolamo, born in 1844, was the son of Salvatore Disparti and Antonina Lucania. Vincenza, my maternal great-grandmother, born in 1847, was the daughter of Nicolo

Sangiorgio and Concetta Saglimbene.

Girolamo and Vincenza had two sons: Giuseppe, Uncle "Joe," born in 1873, and my maternal grandfather, Nicolo, born April 1, 1876. As was the custom, the first-born son Giuseppe was given the name of his paternal grandfather, and Nicolo was named for his maternal grandfather, Nicolo Sangiorgio.

Disparti and Latona Family Tree

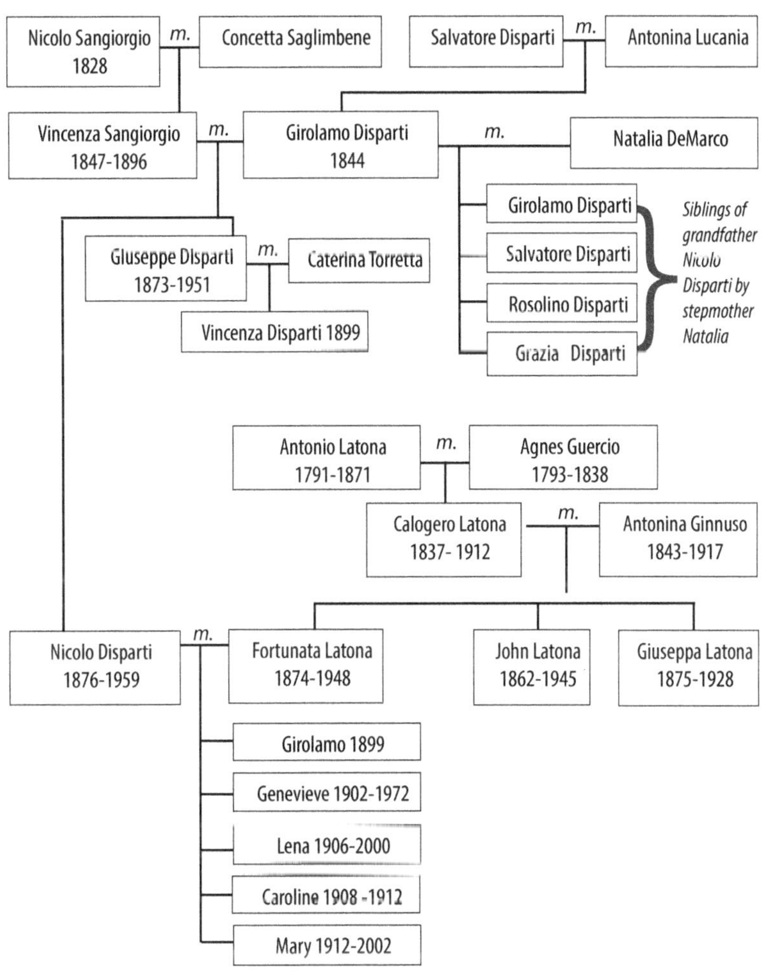

Nicolo Disparti 1876-1959

Joseph Disparti 1873-1951

From left are Grandmother Rose Iannolina Sangiorgio, Nicolo Sangiorgio (1872–1962) (Nicolo Disparti's first cousin, with grandfather Filippo Sangiorgio (1842–1913).

Nicolo Sangiorgio (with blanket on shoulder), Salvatore Sangiorgio on his father Nicolo's lap, mother Angela DiFiore and three daughters. The Sangiorgio family were first cousins of my grandfather, Nicolo Disparti.

Girolamo, Vincenza, Giuseppe and Nicolo lived in a stone house with a heated kitchen and two unheated rooms in the town of Lercara Friddi. Livestock and chickens were kept in a barn attached to the back of their home. Girolamo worked a nearby farm where he raised vegetables and grapes on land located on a terraced hillside overlooking the town. Giuseppe learned to read and write at an early age and excelled in his school work. Nicolo, three years younger, was a slow learner. Both boys were gifted soccer and bocce ball players. Vincenza was a good cook. She was known for using artichokes to complement her entrees and for her fruit pies. When time permitted, she would join Girolamo and the two boys, helping where needed in the fields.

Stone House In Lercara Friddi built in 1650

It is of interest that the Disparti, Latona, Nasca and Galusha families lived in small towns in Northwest Sicily in close proximity to Palermo. Valledolmo was within thirty kilometers, over a range of mountains from Lercara Friddi. Cerda was near the coast and about 30 kilometers from Valledolmo.

Maps depicting the towns of Lercara Friddi, Valledolmo, and Cerda where the Disparti, Latona, Nasca and Galusha families lived.

Map of upstate New York region where many Sicilian immigrants settled.

CHAPTER 2

The Mine Explosion

As the brothers got older, they were recruited to work in the nearby sulfur mine. Because of their size, they were able to make their way through the narrow mine tunnels leading donkey carts loaded with sulfur ore. Other children who did not have families to support them were forced to work as slave laborers in the mines. These children worked six days a week in hazardous conditions, digging out the ore and loading it into the small carts. Many of these youngsters were malnourished and poorly treated by the mine owners and supervisors.

Girolamo Disparti was cultivating artichokes when he heard a loud explosion coming from the sulfur mine about a mile away. That morning, Girolamo had taken his son, Nicolo, age eight, to the mine.

Nicolo had worked in the mine most of the summer and was proud of the money he had earned. He told his father, "I will be finished around four o'clock and will make my way home after work."

Nicolo's job was to lead a small donkey cart loaded with sulfur ore out of the mine. He was chosen for the job because he was strong and short in stature.

Laborers inside a sulfur mine loading a cart

Miners young and old outside of a sulfur mine

As Girolamo and his friend Jacobi approached the entrance to the mine, they were stopped by guards who told them, "There are continued explosions within the mine and the mine is unsafe to enter."

Huge plumes of yellow sulfur-laced air and fiery particles of debris were being discharged, completely obscuring the mine entrance. During the late afternoon, the smoke started to clear and the explosions became less frequent.

A mine superintendent asked for search-and-rescue volunteers. Many people gathered around the mine waiting for news of those trapped inside. Girolamo and Jacobi stood with other volunteers until the superintendent gave the signal that the search and rescue could begin, as darkness was setting in.

Girolamo picked up a stretcher and lantern prior to entering the mine. As they entered the main tunnel, there was a large cave-in that required clearance. Several of the men used shovels and carts to remove the dirt and rocks to allow passage into the main tunnel. The search-and-rescue teams fanned out to access the myriad of narrow branching tunnels that ran through the mine. A few of the cart boys were found alive at the end of the main tunnel.

One of the surviving boys knew Nicolo and said, "I saw him just before the explosion, heading for one of the back tunnels with his donkey cart." After several minutes, Girolamo and Jacobi reached a back tunnel and found Nicolo covered with rocks, dirt and ash, lying beside his donkey and an overturned cart. He was unconscious and appeared to have sustained sulfur burns to his face, chest and upper back. His father, with the help of others, rolled him onto the stretcher and carefully transported him out of the mine.

His mother, Vincenza, had been awaiting the arrival of survivors and was overjoyed to see Nicolo's stretcher. Vincenza pleaded with Nicolo to wake up, but he remained non-responsive as his stretcher was readied for transport to the hospital in Palermo, about forty-five kilometers away. Within a few minutes, he was loaded on a horse-drawn cart with fresh hay for the trip to Palermo. Girolamo and Vincenza followed the wagon to Palermo. When the wagon arrived in the courtyard of the hospital, a priest came out and administered last rites to Nicolo and the others as the wagon was being unloaded. Nicolo was still not responsive after being admitted to the burn ward.

The doctor told Girolamo and Vincenza, "Nicolo might not survive his injuries. There is nothing you can do, so it is best for you both to return home." However, after a few hours, Nicolo started to regain consciousness.

He told the doctor, "My right arm hurts when I move it." In addition to the severe facial burns, he had a broken arm. Of great concern was the proximity of the burns to his right eye and those around his nose. The doctor placed a plaster cast on his broken arm and started daily dressings for his sulfur burns. Each time his dressing was changed, Nicolo would cry out in pain as his burnt skin was peeled off. After a few weeks, there appeared to be some healing of his facial and trunk burns with new skin starting to replace burned skin. At that point, the daily dressing changes were less painful and better tolerated by Nicolo. He also started to eat solid food and walk around the hospital grounds.

After six weeks, his parents came to take Nicolo home. His older brother, Joseph, age eleven, was a great help to his younger brother who was finally getting his strength back. Nicolo had lost his sense of smell and had to wear glasses to improve his poor vision. His lower right eyelid was deformed due to the burn contracture of the eyelid skin. When he returned to the doctor in Palermo for follow-up after three months, he was discharged to return to school. His parents were then told to keep him out of the sulfur mine.

CHAPTER 3

Young Nicolo

Nicolo did not like the classroom. He preferred to be outside doing some type of work. During the summer school recess following the mine explosion, he joined his father each day tending artichokes and soybeans on the family farm. After Nicolo finished primary school at age fourteen, he got a job doing local farm work. Each day he would arise at dawn and dress for a day tending the numerous artichoke and other vegetable fields near his home. He also worked in the vineyards cultivating grapes. His work consisted of hand tilling, weeding, pruning and harvesting the grapes. He learned to graft various grape varieties onto rootstock to provide new plants. He also learned how to make wine.

Lercara Friddi had a soccer team that had won several regional tournaments. Nicolo joined the team as a goalie at age twelve. After a few years he was chosen as the starting goalie. His team placed first in the regional finals and was invited to compete in Palermo in the provincial tournament. Although Nicolo had issues with his eyesight, he had quick reflexes and deflected a number of strikes in the goalie box. His team took first place in the provincial tournament.

Vincenza died a few years after the mine explosion. With two children and his farm to manage, Girolamo needed a new wife. He married Natalie Demarco. The marriage resulted in a dramatic increase in the family with the birth of Girolamo, Salvatore, Rosolino and Grazia.

The barns and loft of the stone house that had provided shelter for the livestock were converted into rooms for the new arrivals. The heated kitchen had a large wood stove and wooden table that could seat eight. Grazia was a very bright girl and excelled in her school work as did her brothers Girolamo and Salvatore. Rosolino, like Nicolo, was more attracted to outdoor pursuits.

CHAPTER 4

Brother Giuseppe

Giuseppe was a very good student. His dedicated efforts came to the attention of the Bishop of Palermo when he arrived to confirm the children in the parish of Santa Maria della Neve. The bishop invited Giuseppe, age twelve, to come to the seminary in Palermo. He would receive an education in Latin, Greek, math, science, philosophy and theology. He was given free tuition, room and board as long as he continued his studies for the priesthood. Giuseppe excelled in his studies and had a bright future as a clergyman in the Roman Catholic Church.

One day, when he was walking around the courtyard of the Cathedral, he saw Bishop Romano and several priests peering down into a large hole. A few minutes later, a winch was brought over to pull out a metal coffin covered with dirt. A crowd of priests and seminarians assembled around the excavation.

After several attempts, the casket was pried open. The interior was filled with gold coins and diamond jewelry. After the gold and diamond jewelry were removed, the casket was closed and returned to its resting place. Bishop Romano and his party followed the bounty into the cathedral. The bishop had everyone sit as he said, "My housekeeper found a letter last week hidden in the rectory's book collection that described the location of a coffin containing gold and fine jewelry buried in the Cathedral Cemetery. I was suspicious that this was a hoax, but my curiosity propelled me to move forward to exhume and open the coffin."

Someone asked, "Bishop, where did these treasures come from?"

He said, "They were given to Bishop Lacava several years ago as 'spoils of war' and he was told to bury them for safekeeping."

Bishop Romano decided to send the jewelry to the Vatican for safekeeping. He planned to distribute the gold coins to the poor of Palermo.

Caterina Toretta had come to Palermo and was staying with friends. She was a bright girl who had finished primary and secondary school in Lercara Friddi. She knew that Giuseppe, Natalia Demarco's stepson, was in Palermo studying for the priesthood and she contacted him.

"I am looking for a secretarial job and would appreciate any help you can give me in finding employment in Palermo," she said. Giuseppe said he would try to help her and would contact her when he had more information.

Giuseppe returned to his dormitory to pick up his books for an afternoon class. After class he went to the library to study. There was a sign posted at the front desk advertising a position in the library. The following day he had to go to the post office in Palermo. While he was in the city, he made contact with Caterina. He told her of the open position at the seminary library. She was most appreciative.

A few weeks later, she was hired for the library job. She was responsible for refilling and stacking the books. Giuseppe saw her almost every day at the library.

After night vespers, he would meet Caterina at her relative's home.

In his last year of study before taking vows to become a priest, Giuseppe began having doubts about committing his life to the Church. Several of his classmates had left the seminary to pursue other careers. Since they had a good education, there were a number of jobs available to them. Some of his seminary friends were involved in local government. Giuseppe decided to leave the seminary and obtain a position in government service. He was able to get a job in the Palermo city government.

CHAPTER 5

The Latona Family

Antonio Latona (1791–1871) and Agnes Guercio (1793–1838) were the parents of Calogero Latona, my great maternal grandfather born in Valledolmo, Sicily on June 24, 1837. His wife Antonina Guinnuso was born June 13, 1843. They were married in 1860 in the Church of Maria SS. della Pietra, where they were both baptized.

Calogero and Antonina had three children: Giovanni Latona, "Uncle John," born in 1862; Fortunata, my maternal grandmother, in 1874; and Giuseppa (Josephina), maternal grand-aunt, in 1875. The family home in Valledolmo was sixty kilometers from Palermo, located in a beautiful valley between two mountain ranges. The verdant farmland was fed by springs and produced grapes, durum wheat and the much-sought-after Siccagno plum tomatoes which were high in nutrients.

Calogero started out as a farmer, then developed a farm labor management business. This required him to travel away from home for long periods of time. Antonina was a full-time homemaker who functioned as both mother and father during Calogero's long absences from home. She did an excellent job in both roles.

There were numerous farms in the small towns in the northwest area of Sicily. Many farm owners contracted out their work to a business that employed farm workers rather than hire their own labor.

In the early 1890s, the government privatized the farms and made farmers pay rent and taxes to use their land. During this time, the Fasci Siciliani movement was started. Fasci, meaning "bundle" in Italian, was an association of laborers that advocated for workers' rights, and it constituted Sicily's first social movement. Calogero's contract farm business was impacted by the movement, making it difficult for him to find workers not allied with Fasci Siciliani.

Their son, Giovanni, exceled in his studies and joined his father in the farm management business. Later, Fortunata joined the company as well. After a few years, Giovanni left to pursue the purchase and management of vacation homes along the northwest coast of Sicily.

Cefalu was a popular winter vacation spot for Europeans fleeing cold winters. Giovanni was a shrewd businessman and purchased several properties to manage. This brought him a very good income. From time to time, he would join his father and sister doing farm management. Sister Giuseppa was completing her primary education when she was recruited to train as a nurse at the Cefalu sanitarium.

Valledolmo, between two mountain ranges

Maternal great-grandfather Calogero Latona (1837–1912)

CHAPTER 6

Nicolo Joins Calogero Latona

Nicolo signed on to work as a field hand with Calogero's team of workers. It did not take long before Nicolo's skills and work ethic were noticed by company management. Each day after work, Nicolo would report to Calogero on the work he and his crew had done.

One day, a young blonde girl was sitting in her father's office as Nicolo came in to make his report.
It was Fortunata. After Nicolo left, Calogero passed the information to Fortunata who recorded it in a large leather-bound journal.

Fortunata Latona
Disparti, maternal
grandmother
(1847-1948)

A few weeks later, Nicolo was called into the office to meet with Calogero about some of his reports. There was some concern about the number of bushels of artichokes that Nicolo had recorded as picked and the number that had been received by the buyer.

Nicolo told Calogero, "I stand by my figures, and I have personally counted each day's harvest before and after it was delivered to the warehouse."

Calogero told him, "If there are any future discrepancies with your numbers, you will be dismissed."

The next day, Nicolo stayed late to recount the number of bushels of artichokes picked by his crew. He then followed them to the warehouse, where they were to be stored. The warehouse manager did not recount or check the delivery.

It was late in the day, but Nicolo decided to stay near the warehouse on the hunch that someone was going to remove some of the bushels. Sometime after dark, a wagon pulled up to the back of the warehouse and several bushels of artichokes were loaded onto the suspicious wagon and it was driven off.

The following day, Nicolo was called in by Calogero who told him, "According to the warehouse manager, your count was wrong again, so you are no longer needed here."

Nicolo then recounted what he had witnessed the previous night at the warehouse. Calogero got very angry and said, "I don't believe you, Nicolo."

However, he wanted the truth, so he told Nicolo, "You go back to work, recount the day's harvest, and report what you find." When he returned after work, Fortunata was there.

Calogero told Nicolo, "Go with Fortunata to the warehouse to recount the bushels."

When they got to the warehouse, Nicolo and Fortunata did a recount and found that Nicolo's figures reported that afternoon to her father were correct.

However, they both noticed that the warehouse manager seemed nervous and wanted them out of the warehouse as soon as they did their recount. Rather than leave the area, Nicolo and Fortunata stayed around. About an hour later, a wagon pulled up and several bushels of the artichokes picked by Nicolo's crew were taken out of the warehouse and loaded onto a wagon.

Fortunata told Nicolo, "We'd better follow the wagon to see where the artichokes you picked end up."

A few minutes later, the wagon stopped at another warehouse and the driver was paid off after he unloaded the stolen bushels of artichokes.

Later that evening, Nicolo and Fortunata returned to her father's office. Calogero was furious that they were so late in returning. He was about to grab Nicolo by the neck and strangle him when Fortunata stepped in, put her hand up and said, "Stop."

She then told Calogero, "We saw the warehouse manager pay off the wagon driver to transport several bushels of artichokes that had been picked by Nicolo's crew to another warehouse."

The next day, Nicolo and Calogero went to see Carmine, the owner of the warehouse. Calogero recounted what Nicolo and Fortunata had seen the night before. Calogero and Nicolo took Carmine by the arm and marched him off to the warehouse where they found a number of bushels of artichokes missing that Nicolo's group had picked the day before. Calogero said to Carmine, "What did you do with the missing bushels of artichokes?"

The nervous manager said, "I am responsible for the thefts. I sold them to a buyer from Palermo."

Carmine asked Calogero for forgiveness and then he handed him an envelope containing the money that he had received for the stolen artichokes.

A few weeks later, Calogero and Fortunata moved on to a new town to supervise another harvest. Nicolo stayed in Lercara Friddi to help with the fava bean harvest. In the fall and winter, Nicolo kept busy doing repairs on the town streets and buildings. He looked forward to returning to the artichoke fields and vineyards in the spring, enjoying the work outside.

CHAPTER 7
Nicolo's Promotion

During the fall harvest, Nicolo was approached by a tall well-dressed man by the name of Salvatore Russo, from Corleone, a mountainous agricultural area in the southwest of Sicily. He asked Nicolo, "Would you work as a supervisor on my ranch?" Nicolo was interested, but before he decided to leave his comfortable lifestyle in Lercara Friddi, he wanted to visit Corleone and see the operation firsthand. The ranch extended for many hectares along the hills and valleys. The vineyards were located on terraced soil on the sides of steep hills. There were sheep, beef cattle and horses. Nicolo had little experience with cattle and horses, but was very interested in the vineyards. Salvatore offered him room, meals and a monthly salary. Sunday would be a day of rest and leisure.

Upon his return to Lercara Friddi, Nicolo asked his father Girolamo, "Do you think I should consider taking the ranch job in Corleone?"

Girolamo said, "It sounds like a good opportunity for you. You should give it a try. You can always return here if you find the job is not to your liking."

At first, Nicolo was a little lonely, having to leave his family and friends in Lercara Friddi. But after a few weeks, he got into his new job and was busy learning how to manage his crew of workers and the livestock. Each day he set aside some time to work in the vineyards. This was his great interest and provided him with a lot of personal satisfaction.

The grape harvest that fall was not as good as expected. Nicolo and Salvatore were disappointed with the inferior harvest and poor quality of the grapes. Nicolo told Salvatore, "I need to spend more time in the vineyards and cultivate other varieties of grapes that I am familiar with, and that I have grown in Lercara Friddi."

In order to obtain these new varieties of plants, it was necessary for Nicolo to graft them onto new rootstock. This was a tedious project which demanded concentration and attention to detail to ensure that the new varieties of grapes were properly placed onto the rootstock. A good number of vigorous new vines resulted from his grafting. They were nurtured and protected until they were ready to stake and trellis. The following year's harvest was much better. The new grape varieties that had been grafted were thriving. Nicolo was an excellent wine maker and preferred to use one varietal of grape rather than to blend several types of grapes to make his red table wine and his white wine he called "champagna."

The cattle and horse operations were doing well. Nicolo was happy with his job but missed his family and friends, especially Fortunata.

During his third year on the job, Nicolo ran into Calogero, who was passing through Corleone on his way to another job. Calogero told Nicolo that he was having trouble with the farm workers that were members of the Fasci Siciliani. The Fasci were farm workers who banded together to obtain better pay and jobs. Calogero was having a hard time finding qualified workers since many of his former workers were now Fasci members working under union rules. These labor issues were destined to cause continued disputes for several more years.

CHAPTER 8
Mafia Executions

That evening as Calogero, Nicolo and Fortunata were finishing dinner, they heard gunshots. The Corleone area was the home of several Mafia members. They were known for violence and extortion. Earlier, the Mafia had rounded up several members of the Corleone Fasci Siciliani after they attended a meeting with Bernardo Verra, their leader. The Mafia chief lined up a number of the Fasci members before a firing squad and shot them. Their leader Bernardo escaped.

Early the next morning, Calogero, Fortunata and Nicolo left Corleone for Lercara Friddi. On the way out of town, they were stopped by armed Mafia operatives and taken to a house where they were detained for questioning.

They asked Calogero, "Are you a member of Fasci Siciliani?" and he responded, "No."

After several hours, the Mafia chief came to the house and told his men, "Lock these people up for further questioning."

After an anxious night, they were taken to another house for further interrogation. They were each asked, "Did you see the murders in Corleone?" They answered that they had not seen them. That answer seemed to satisfy the Mafia chief and he had them released.

Calogero was greatly shaken by the detainment and

questioning and decided to lay low in Corleone for a few days before returning home. Fortunata stayed with her father. Nicolo returned to the ranch in Corleone.

When Nicolo returned, Salvatore asked, "Where have you been these last few days? We have missed you." Nicolo replied that he had been locked up overnight by the Mafia after the executions in Corleone.

Salvatore told Nicolo to stay at the ranch and not return to the town of Corleone. Salvatore had also been questioned by the Mafia about his involvement in the Fasci Siciliani movement.

After a few weeks, Nicolo decided to return to Lercara Friddi on Sunday to see his parents. Girolamo told him that he had been recruited to join the local Fasci Siciliani group but had refused. Girolamo owned his land and did not need to pay rent or taxes to the government. However, he was very concerned that in a short time, he would have his land annexed by the government and would be required to pay rent and taxes.

CHAPTER 9

Nicolo Accepts Calogero's Offer

That evening, Calogero returned to Lercara Friddi with Fortunata and stopped by Girolamo's house. Nicolo was about to leave when they arrived. Calogero was still quite agitated regarding the Mafia encounter. He told Nicolo," I am so upset with what is going on that I am ready to quit." He asked Nicolo, "Will you rejoin Fortunata and me? We need your help to continue the farm management business."

Nicolo said, "I will think about the offer, but I need to return to the ranch tonight." The next week, Nicolo decided to accept Calogero's offer. He was upset about leaving his newly established vineyards in Corleone, but he missed Fortunata. He told Salvatore that there were problems at home, and he needed to return to Lercara Friddi. He promised he would come back in the fall to help with the harvest of the grapes he had grafted and cultivated.

Instead of reporting to Calogero, he and Fortunata would work as the leadership team. She would be manning the office and doing the payroll and Nicolo would be in charge of hiring and supervising the workers.

On his first day back, he reconnected with Fortunata who brought him up to date on what he needed to do. His first chore was to hand-pick his crew of workers. This turned out to be more difficult than he expected, since a number of his friends and former coworkers had joined the

Fasci Siciliani movement. After a few days, he was able to gather a handful of new workers to harvest the artichoke and fava bean crop. The harvest was good and management was pleased.

Fortunata was a good manager and was well-liked by the workers. She was an attractive young lady with blue eyes and blond hair. She did have a problem with asthma, which kept her inside and resulted in occasional trips to the doctor for treatment.

Every few weeks, her father would visit, and she would report to him on the farm operation. On occasion, Calogero would ask Nicolo to join him and his daughter for dinner. He told Nicolo, "I am going to retire." He was still concerned about the government annexation of land, the Fasci Siciliani movement and the Mafia. He was interested in moving to America, "Where the streets are paved with gold."

During the Feast of the Assumption, the town had a religious holiday. In the evening, after dinner, dancing began on the town square. Nicolo spotted Fortunata and asked her to dance the tarantella. Nicolo was wearing a dark blue suit with a white shirt and tie. She was surprised he was such a good dancer.

In September, Nicolo took a few weeks away from his supervising duties in Lercara Friddi to check on the vineyards at the ranch in Corleone, as he had promised Salvatore. He was surprised to see that his vines had produced an abundance of quality grapes and suggested to Salvatore that they make wine. After a few days of harvesting, Nicolo set about crushing and pressing the grapes and transferring the juice into oaken barrels for fermenting.

When Nicolo returned to Lercara Friddi, Calogero told him that while he was gone, things had not gone well in the fields and several of the workers had not reported to work. Calogero had not been able to get the crew back to work, and they had fallen behind in the fall harvest. With no one else to turn to for help, Fortunata was very happy to have Nicolo back. He quickly got the men back into the fields and the crops harvested. What had been assumed lost, was regained by Nicolo's leadership.

CHAPTER 10

Nicolo Turns Twenty-one

On April 1, 1897, Nicolo turned twenty-one. His father, Girolamo, stepmother Natalie, and Calogero, Antonina and Fortunata planned a birthday party for him and invited his friends and coworkers. The party was held in the Lercara Friddi town square with music, dancing, food and wine. Tables were filled with grilled vegetables, meats, pastas and desserts. Fortunata and Nicolo enjoyed the food and wine and danced the tarantella with their friends. The party lasted late into the mild spring evening.

As the party was breaking up, Fortunata started to wheeze as the cooler night air moved into the town square. She had difficulty breathing. She was taken to a friend's house nearby. A ring of garlic was placed on her neck, and she tried to inhale hot tea vapors, but her breathing did not improve. The local town doctor was called. He gave her additional medicines but the asthma attack persisted. After a few hours the doctor advised that she be transported to a hospital in Palermo.

Nicolo and Calogero secured a covered cart and two horses and drove Fortunata to the hospital in Palermo for treatment. When she arrived at the hospital, she was turning blue and losing consciousness. The medical staff immediately started to resuscitate her. They removed secretions from her airway, that she could not expel, with long rubber suction bulbs passed in and out of her mouth and upper airway. Her color and breathing started to improve after the suctioning. She was given a dose of ipecac to induce vomiting to empty her stomach and make breathing easier. Hot tea vapors, belladonna and a small dose of opium were given to sedate her. After several hours, the asthma attack subsided and she was able to once again breath without difficulty. After a few days of rest, she was able to return home.

A few nights later, Fortunata had another asthma attack, but this one was not as severe and did not last as long. Calogero decided that it would be best for Fortunata to return home to Valledolmo. The town was near the coast on the Ligurian Sea. The salt air would be good for her. Fortunata left the next day for the coast in a horse drawn carriage. She was excited to return home.

For a few days, Fortunata stayed in bed to regain her strength after the long carriage ride from the mountains to Valledolmo. Her sister Giuseppa brought her meals to her out on the veranda where she could breathe the fresh warm sea air. After a few days of rest, Fortunata and Giuseppa traveled to the beach on a bright sunny day in late April. The sisters decided to cool off in the ocean waters after a few hours in the sun. The cool water triggered another asthma attack which was fortunately of short duration. The next day, Giuseppa took Fortunata to the Cefalu Sanitarium where she worked as a nurse. The Sanitarium was renowned for the treatment of patients with respiratory diseases and tuberculosis.

Carlo Nasca was the young doctor who was assigned to see Fortunata. After reviewing her past history and treatment, he spent a good deal of time listening to her lungs through a large tube that he placed on various locations on the front and back of her chest. Carlo was able to hear sounds called rales that were indicative of pneumonia, and he recommended that Fortunata be admitted for treatment. Giuseppa stayed with Fortunata until after dinner and then returned home. To her surprise, Calogero greeted her as she entered the house. He had been worried about Fortunata and decided to return home to check on her.

Giuseppa said, "I just left Fortunata at the Cefalu Sanitarium. She has pneumonia in addition to her asthma."

Calogero asked, "How bad is she, and is she in any danger of dying?"

Giuseppa said, "She is sick, but the doctor felt she was in the early stages of her pneumonia and there is a good chance that she will respond well to treatment."

The next day Giuseppa and Calogero visited Fortunata in the sanitarium, located on the coast and surrounded by parks with trees and grass. Fortunata had been moved out to the open porch facing the ocean to enjoy the fresh salt air. She had been given a mixture of garlic, fava bean and sulfur to take for her pneumonia. Brewer's yeast, rich in B vitamins, was added to her diet. She was instructed in deep-breathing exercises, which she did with some difficulty because they would induce spells of coughing. Twice a day, a nurse would do chest percussion to facilitate her expelling retained secretions. Each day she felt better and was able to breathe easier. After a month's stay, she was released to go home with her sister and father.

CHAPTER 11

Giovanni and Agnes Latona

When Fortunata returned home, her brother Giovanni Latona had come with his wife Agnes for a visit. Agnes was Giovanni's first cousin. There was some concern about the marriage since they were first cousins, but they had the blessings of the Church. They had recently married and were planning to go to America.

Giovanni had sold some prime seacoast homes around Cefalu and had money for travel. He was hoping to buy land in America and grow grapes. He had a friend, Antonio Battaglia that had immigrated to a small town in western New York, Geneseo, and had opened a bar and restaurant, the M & B, with another Sicilian, Tony D'Aprile. Antonio was willing to sponsor Giovanni and Agnes.

M & B, bar and restaurant on Court Street, Geneseo, New York

Within a few days, they were planning to board a ship out of Palermo harbor for transport to New York. After a rough crossing in steerage class, aboard the ship Bolivia, they arrived with other Sicilians at Ellis Island in late May of 1897. Those in steerage class slept on the floor with no privacy, poor ventilation and limited facilities. Such was the fate of those passengers ticketed in the lowest transport class.

Photo of a steerage class section

After their arrival in New York, each passenger was given a through medical examination prior to disembarking the ship. If there was any question of their health status, they were placed in a two-week quarantine. Fortunately, both Giovanni and Agnes passed their initial examination and were released to travel. Antonio Battaglia was there to meet them and accompany them from Ellis Island to Geneseo.

Giovanni bought seven acres of land from Tony D'Aprile on 56 Court Street along New York State Route 63, which passed through the town of Geneseo and across the Genesee River a short distance from his land. They lived with the Battaglias in a room over the restaurant until their home was completed.

Giovanni hired a crew to assist him with plowing up the ground and planting grapes on his seven acres. Giovanni and Agnes learned to speak English, became active in the small-town community and became American citizens. They helped build and attended St. Mary's Catholic Church, a short walk up the hill from their home. Giovanni started selling his grapes to local wineries. His grapes were in great demand, and he sold out his

St. Mary's Church - Geneseo, N.Y.

crop each year. With the money from his grape sales, he leased additional land and started new vineyards.

Rather than work his vineyards, Giovanni hired men to do the tilling, pruning and cultivating. Each fall he would hire the local school children to help harvest the grapes. This was a most innovative idea. After a full day of harvesting grapes, the children were treated to dinner with cake and ice cream.

Fortunata, her sister-in-law Agnes Latona, and her brother John Latona with Lena Nasca and Gen Disparti standing

Giovanni wrote to Calogero and told him to consider coming to New York. There was land available if he wanted to farm and raise grapes. Calogero wrote back and said that he was very concerned with the government annexing land, the Fasci Siciliani movement and the Mafia. He would like to come to New York but his health was failing. He was considering retiring and turning his contract farm business over to Fortunata and Nicolo.

Uncle Joe Disparti, Uncle John Latona and Nicolo Disparti checking on the grapes

CHAPTER 12

Prizzi

Calogero was supervising a large farm operation near the town of Prizzi when Fortunata returned from Valledolmo. She was doing well after her bout of pneumonia and attacks of asthma. She was responsible for keeping a list of the workers, their hours and payroll, in addition to monitoring the number of bushels of crop picked and delivered to the warehouses. Because of the variety of crops and the different dates for harvesting, she had to spend a good deal of time in and around the fields and storage warehouses, which was not good for her delicate health.

Calogero hired Antonio Sparacio to help Fortunata with the outside harvest counting and monitoring the warehouse deliveries. Antonio had finished secondary school and was reliable and accurate with his production counts. Keeping up with the local warehouse storage was a challenge, since once the crop was delivered, there was no one to oversee it. Too often, some of the stored crop would be stolen. The warehouse managers were rarely reliable and took no responsibility for securing their warehouses. Good workers were hard to recruit and keep. The Mafia and the theft of portions of the crop stored in the warehouse placed a great deal of stress on farm managers like Calogero.

In spite of these difficulties and challenges, Calogero and Fortunata enjoyed the work and continued to travel to towns that needed their services. The work paid well, and they enjoyed making friends in these small rural towns. Antonio and Fortunata worked well together, and they were often seen in the Prizzi town square enjoying music and wine in the afternoons after work. Antonio's family had a restaurant which was famous for its fine cuisine. People would come to Prizzi from the surrounding towns to enjoy the food and entertainment provided by the Sparacios. Calogero and Fortunata were frequent customers.

CHAPTER 13

Girolamo is Injured

Things had been going well in Lercara Friddi. Great-grand-father Girolamo and his wife Natalia's young family were attending primary school.

On his way into town, Girolamo's cart turned a corner, hit a large rock and flipped over on its side. Girolamo's right leg was pinned under the wheel of the overturned cart. After a few minutes, help arrived. Several men turned the cart upright and released the pressure on Girolamo's broken leg. He was taken to Palermo for treatment. Surgeons at the hospital determined that the leg bones were broken in several places. The foot and ankle were blue and his pulses could not be felt. There was a good chance his leg would require amputation.

A young surgeon, Ricardo, felt his leg could be saved. The deformed leg was gradually straightened as Ricardo applied manual traction to his foot and ankle. The injured leg was placed in a traction device with two metal bars joined at the top, and wool pads secured to the bars to support his leg. Weights were added to ropes attached to the metal frame to keep the leg suspended, balanced and elevated.

After a short time, the circulation of the foot and ankle improved. Girolamo was fortunate that he had sustained no lacerations or open wounds, so infection was not a consideration. After three weeks in suspended traction, he was taken to a large room where he was given something to breathe which caused him to lose consciousness while the surgeons further straightened his broken leg and placed him in a cast from his toes to his groin.

A few days later, he was lifted off his bed and placed in a wooden chair with wheels that had an extension to support his fractured leg. He was taken outside to breathe the fresh air from the Bay of Palermo. He was placed in parallel bars and instructed in walking with wooden crutches. After a few days, he was able to get himself out of bed into a chair and walk to the bathroom. He was told not to put weight on the fractured leg. After a few more weeks, his cast was removed, and he had another toe-to-groin cast applied, He was told he could go home.

Nicolo had taken a leave of absence from his work with Calogero and Fortunata so that he could tend his father's crops and assist his stepmother Natalie with the children. After the major crops were harvested, he found work repairing the town's stone walkways in late fall and winter. The money he earned from the recently harvested crops and his wages from the town kept the family going while his father, Girolamo, recovered from his broken leg.

At six months, Girolamo was able to get back in the fields and supervise his farm workers. After his work was finished, Nicolo would come over to help his dad and his stepbrother Rosolino with their crops.

Rosolino Disparti and Nicolo Disparti

CHAPTER 14

Bocce Tournament

Giuseppe and Nicolo had been avid bocce ball players in Lercara Friddi. Each year there was a bocce championship held in Palermo in late November. Teams from all over Sicily came to compete in the weekend matches for prizes and money.

Nicolo played with some of his workers each weekend. His team enjoyed drinks and dinner after competing in their town matches each weekend. In spite of his eye problem, Nicolo had a great bocce toss and would often win a match with the closest toss to the white rabbit ball. He and his team entered the November Palermo Bocce Tournament. Giuseppe, now a government worker for the city of Palermo, also entered his bocce team into the tournament.

There were forty-eight teams that qualified to compete on the city's sixteen bocce courts, which were constructed of wood sides with hard-packed sand for the playing surface. Judges, rather than players, were used to measure the closeness of the four colored balls to the rabbit and to award earned points. The first team getting twelve points was declared the winner of the match. To progress to the next level, a team needed to win three of its five matches.

Nicolo's and Giuseppe's teams did very well and moved up the ladder to the finals. Wagers were placed on the teams by the gallery and the matches began at noon.

Giuseppe's team of office workers were dressed in uniforms bearing Palermo City logos. Nicolo's team was dressed in brown pants and blue shirts with the yellow lion insignia of Lercara Friddi on their backs.

As expected, the match was a seesaw event, with both teams tied at three wins each going into the final matches. Giuseppe's team won the fourth match by a point. Nicolo's team won the fifth match. Because it was getting dark, the judges announced that whichever team won the next match would be declared the winner. Nicolo was picked by his teammates to be the last bowler. Both teams traded the lead as the match progressed to even at 11-11. Giuseppe would face off against Nicolo in the race to win the winning point in the winner-take-all match. Both teams rolled balls very close to the rabbit, but Nicolo's was closest and his team was declared the winner of the Palermo City Bocce Tournament. Nicolo's team was presented the trophy and 10,000 lire. Extra money was picked up from the local wagering.

After the match, Nicolo invited Giuseppe's team for drinks. After a few drinks, Giuseppe told Nicolo, "I am being drafted into the Army and will need to leave Palermo and my wife." The military deployment would last three years.

CHAPTER 15

Nicolo And Fortunata Team Up

Nicolo rejoined Calogero to manage a crew of Lercara Friddi farm workers. He liked being at home and continued to help his father and younger brothers with their crops. Girolamo was doing well but still needed help with difficult projects. His young sons, Girolamo, Salvatore and Rosolino, were in school except for the weekends. Rosolino looked forward to working with his father and Nicolo on Saturday. He caught on quickly to the chores but seemed to tire after a few hours of work. However, as he grew, his endurance improved, and he was able to work a full day. Salvatore and Girolamo were more interested in school than farming and rarely worked in the fields.

While Fortunata was at the Sanitarium in Cefalu, she spent time with a nurse who taught her how to evaluate common injuries and illnesses. She was a natural healer and had a God-given talent that she humbly used. She instinctively knew how to care for the sick and injured. She listened attentively to the patient and usually was able to provide a remedy. This skill came in handy while managing the farm workers, who sustained injuries from falls on the steep hills and were brought to her for triage.

Using her sensitive fingers, she could detect the abnormal movement along the course of a bone indicative of a fracture. If she detected a fracture, she would have the injured worker transported to a bonesetter or surgeon for treatment. For those with lesser injuries, she would apply splints and supports that she made out of wood padded with soft wool. She also taught those suffering from repetitive occupational injuries how to stretch and strengthen the affected body part to avoid reinjury.

Fortunata saw Nicolo each day and on weekends they spent time together. Nicolo continued to be well-liked by his workers. Calogero gave him more responsibility for making day-to-day decisions in managing the farm workers. Often Nicolo and Fortunata would be on their own with Calogero out of town managing other farms. The harvests were extremely busy times, and it was often necessary to hire children to pick the crops, especially the grapes, which demanded to be harvested at just the right time or risk ruin and financial loss.

CHAPTER 16

Giuseppe Disparti is Drafted

In Sicily, a male of eighteen was placed on the conscription list unless there was some reason for being excluded, such as poor eyesight, a chronic medical condition that required treatment, or some physical or mental disability. Giuseppe's name came up for active military service as required of all able-bodied Sicilian males.

During the last decade of the 1800s, a number of families left Sicily to relocate to South America and the United States. This exodus of young males caused a tremendous void in the military which did not meet its yearly quota of recruits.

When Giuseppe reported to his draft board, he was given a written examination and marksman's test to determine the best place for him in the army. He scored very high in the written test and was an outstanding marksman. He was made a junior officer and sent to gunnery school. After three months, he was promoted to instructor in the use of rifles and carbines. He liked teaching his new recruits and was well-liked. He taught them how to clean their weapons, adjust the gun sights, and calm their breathing and movements when aiming. Giuseppe instructed them in compensating for the wind and its effect on the path of the gun's projectile.

Each day he would arrange for his class to have a

shooting competition on the range after training was done. His recruits liked to place bets on the participants. After the competition, the bets would be settled. Marco, one of the trainees, was a good shot and challenged Giuseppe to a match. The targets would be set at 100 meters, and they each would have ten shots. The targets were drawings of a man's chest with the heart outlined in red. After the rounds were completed, Marco's targets were examined. He hit the heart nine out of ten times. Giuseppe hit the heart all ten times. Giuseppe was awarded several medals for his marksmanship during his years in service.

His wife, Caterina, continued to work in Palermo during Giuseppe's deployment. She had been promoted to an assistant librarian at the seminary. During the early part of his army service, he found time to return home at least once a month. Later on, his visits became less frequent.

During his last year in the army, Caterina became pregnant. A blue-eyed blond daughter, Vincenzia, was born later that year. When Giuseppe returned from his obligatory service, he was given back his government job. He was required to spend two weekends a month away in the army reserve, which caused a great deal of marital distress.

CHAPTER 17

Nicolo Marries Fortunata

After a full day of work harvesting the fava bean and artichoke crops, Nicolo asked Calogero, "Can I speak to you about Fortunata?" Calogero put his hand on Nicolo's shoulder and walked with him into his office. Fortunata had left to prepare dinner.

Nicolo said, "I want to marry Fortunata, but before I ask her, I want your permission."

Calogero asked, "Can you provide for her?"

Nicolo said, "I can provide for her with the money I have earned working with you and from my grapes."

Calogero then embraced Nicolo and said," I am delighted to have you as the husband of my Fortunata. You are an honest, hardworking and talented young man."

Later that evening after dinner, Nicolo approached Fortunata in the kitchen and asked her, "Will you marry me? I have spoken with your father today and he gave me his blessing."

Fortunata was in tears as she said, "Yes, Nicolo, I will marry you."

Calogero came into the kitchen with glasses of home-made limoncello to toast the bride and groom-to-be.

The wedding was held in the beautiful old church of SS della Purita in June of 1897. A former classmate of Giuseppe's, Bartolomeo Ricotta, was the pastor of della

Purita, and he agreed to marry Nicolo and Fortunata. In addition to the immediate family, there were a number of guests in attendance. Fortunata's sister, Giuseppa, was the maid of honor. Nicolo's half-sister Grazia was the flower girl. Giuseppe was best man, and Nicolo's half-brothers Salvatore, Rosolino and Girolamo were groomsmen. Following the wedding and reception, the bridal couple was off to Taormina, Sicily, for a week's honeymoon.

Calogero (Jerry) Disparti, first and only son of Nicolo and Fortunata, was born in Sicily in 1900. He was named after his grandfather as was the custom. Calogero Latona had considered retiring and moving to America to join his son Giovanni who had immigrated to Geneseo, New York with his wife Agnes in 1897. Giovanni and Agnes Latona had no children.

However, Calogero was not sure he was ready to give up his farm management business, and he approached Nicolo about going to America. Initially, Nicolo was reluctant to consider a move, but after talking with several friends who had relatives in America, he decided to go. The government was annexing more land, and it was more difficult to recruit good farm workers. His grapes in Corleone were thriving, but the heavy Mafia presence there kept Nicolo away.

CHAPTER 18

Nicolo Goes to America

A paid sponsor was arranged to meet Nicolo in New York and get him a job in America. Because of his poor eyesight and lack of smell, he was sent first class rather than steerage. First-class passengers were usually not quarantined, did not have to go through a medical examination, and were not delayed on arrival at Ellis Island, as were the underclasses.

Nicolo boarded a steamship in Palermo in 1900. As the vessel was leaving the harbor, a fire started in the engine room. Other boats provided assistance in safely transferring the passengers and their baggage back to port. Nicolo contacted his brother Giuseppe after he returned to port, and he came to the Port of Palermo to pick him up.

Nicolo stayed with Caterina and Giuseppe until he was given passage on another ship bound for New York's Ellis Island. During his stay in Palermo, he asked Giuseppe, "Would you be interested in coming to New York after I get settled?" Giuseppe said, "I would find it difficult to leave Caterina and Vincenzia. As you can see, we are having some issues, and I am still required to do my two weekends a month reserve time."

The two-week trip to New York was uneventful aboard the steamship Marco Minghetti. He arrived at Ellis Island on May 15, 1900.

S.S. MARCO MINGHETTI, 1876 Italia Line
Courtesy The Peabody Museum of Salem

Nicolo traveled by train to Rochester, then by wagon to Geneseo. He lived with his brother-in-law Giovanni Latona and his wife Agnes in their Court Street house. In payment for his transport to New York, he was contracted to work at the Retsof salt mine.

The Retsof salt mine, off State Route 63 in Livingston County, was ten miles from Geneseo. It was the largest salt mine in the world and produced 18,000 tons of rock salt per day. The harvested rock salt was transported on the small Genesee-Wyoming railroad to the main lines in neighboring towns. Horse-drawn carts took Nicolo to the Retsof salt mine each day with other recently arrived immigrants from Geneseo, Mount Morris and other neighboring towns.

CHAPTER 19

Nicolo Found Unconscious

After Nicolo had worked a few weeks in the salt mine, a gas leak developed, sending the miners running out of the mine for their safety. Because of Nicolo's lack of smell, he had no sense that there was a leak. He was found later by coworkers passed out from the toxic gas. He was carried out of the mine and gradually regained consciousness in the fresh air. When he was fully awake, the superintendent said, "Nicolo, you are a good worker, but being unable to smell makes me have to let you go from the salt mine to a safer job."

Nicolo returned home to Geneseo without a job. Giovanni, who was on the town board of directors, found Nicolo a job as a laborer for the town of Geneseo. Nicolo had some experience with stone and cement sidewalk repairs and was assigned to assist with mixing and pouring the concrete for the new sidewalks being constructed on both sides of Court and Main Streets. He also installed large concrete drainage pipes that would carry rain and snow runoff from the center of town to the Genesee River at the end of Court Street. He learned to install street lights. In the spring, after his town job, he helped Giovanni's crew tend the several acres of grapes on Giovanni's land.

Nicolo had brought grape cuttings to Geneseo to graft as he had done in Sicily. These cultivars were grafted onto local root stock to plant in the fertile soil adjacent to the Genesee River. Giovanni Latona had seven acres of grapes in fields just east of his house on Court Street. After work with the Town of Geneseo, Nicolo would cultivate row after row of those vines using hand tools.

CHAPTER 20

Fortunata and Jerry Come to Geneseo

On April 16, 1902, Fortunata and son Jerry came to Geneseo to join Nicolo. They came steerage class, disembarking at Ellis Island. Fortunata had a cousin who lived near New York City who met them at Ellis Island and helped her and Jerry with transportation by train to Avon, New York, about twenty miles from Geneseo.

Nicolo and Giovanni met them in Avon. They were about five miles from Geneseo when the rear axle of their wagon broke. Nicolo had borrowed the wagon from a friend. Giovanni stayed with his sister and little Jerry. Nicolo walked to Geneseo to get another wagon. On his way into Geneseo, he was picked up by Tony D'Aprile who volunteered to fetch the stranded passengers and bring them to Geneseo. Nicolo latter found a friend to repair the broken axle so he could get the borrowed cart back to the owner.

The young Disparti family lived with Giovanni and Agnes on Court Street until Nicolo had enough money to buy a house, across the street at 37 Court Street. A few years later, in 1904, Genevieve was born, followed by Lena in 1906, Caroline in 1908 and Mary, the youngest, in 1912. Caroline died at age four of meningitis. Nicolo became a citizen of the United States in 1911 in Geneseo. Tony D'Aprile was his sponsor.

Jerry, Nicolo, Lena, Mary in highchair, Fortunata, Caroline and Genevieve Disparti

The Disparti children attended grade and high school under the guidance of the faculty and student teachers of the Geneseo Normal School. The school was located within a short distance of their home. It later would become the University of New York Campus at Geneseo.

The house on Court Street had a large kitchen, dining room, bathroom and parlor on the first floor and three bedrooms on the second floor. Although there was only one bathroom, somehow, they managed. Chamber pots were placed in each bedroom and emptied daily. There was a large earthen basement for storage of garlic, vegetables and several barrels of wine. The home had a rear and front porch surrounded by an acre of land. Nicolo had several fruit trees and a vegetable garden in the back yard. A large Seckel pear tree graced the front yard near the street. In late August, it provided many sweet pears for the grandkids to harvest.

CHAPTER 21

Giuseppe Disparti Comes to Geneseo

After his discharge from the Army, Giuseppe returned to his home in Palermo with his wife, Caterina and their daughter, Vincenzia. After the rigorous but carefree life in the military, Giuseppe became bored with his office job and with married life. He contacted Giovanni Latona and his brother Nicolo about coming to join them in Geneseo. He had saved enough money to buy ship passage and purchase land. He did not require a sponsor.

His plan was to come to Geneseo, buy some land and start vineyards of his own. He sailed out of Palermo in the spring of 1903 and arrived at Ellis Island three weeks later. Brother-in-law Giovanni Latona and Tony Battaglia met him at Ellis Island and traveled with him to Geneseo.

When he arrived in Geneseo, Nicolo was happy to be reunited with his brother who provided him a place to stay in his house at 37 Court Street. Fortunata had young Jerry, age two, to look after and was overwhelmed with Giuseppe's constant demands for clean clothes and meals.

She told Nicolo, "Giuseppe needs to find his own place to live."

Nicolo took his brother aside and told him, "You need to find your own place to live. You are causing a great deal of extra work for Fortunata, who is pregnant."

Giuseppe found a five-acre tract of land on the east

side of upper Court Street with a stone house and suitable location to plant grapes. Nicolo supplied his brother with grafted root stock he had been saving for him in anticipation of his move to the States. Nicolo and Giovanni's crew helped Giuseppe till his land and plant the grape stock.

Although he was not a farmer, Giuseppe enjoyed the challenge of growing the Concord, Niagara and Delaware grapes and learned to be an excellent wine maker. After a few years, Nicolo suggested that he bring his wife and daughter to America, but this never occurred.

CHAPTER 22

Calogero and Antonina Latona come to Geneseo

The farm management business was becoming increasingly difficult due to the shortage of men willing to work in the fields, the increasing government tariffs and controls, plus the escalating Mafia presence. Farm owners were cancelling their contracts with Calogero.

Antonio Sparacio from Prizzi heard that Calogero might be going to America. The Sparacio family trattoria was doing well, and they were looking for additional business opportunities. Antonio had enjoyed the work he had done with Calogero and Fortunata and was interested in returning to the farm contract business.

After returning to Valledolmo and talking with Antonina about their future plans, Calogero decided to write Giovanni and Fortunata about coming to Geneseo.

A few weeks later, Antonio Sparacio made an offer to buy Calogero's contract farm business, and he accepted.

Giovanni, Fortunata, and sister Giuseppa who lived in Geneseo with her husband, Joseph Aprile, were overjoyed about their parents' decision to come to America.

Calogero was sixty-nine and Antonina sixty-three when they departed from the Port of Naples for New York City.

Giovanni was at Ellis Island to meet his parents and take them by train to Avon, New York, and they were transported from there to Geneseo by Nicolo in a horse-drawn wagon.

Fortunata prepared a room for them on the first floor in the spacious parlor of the Court Street house.

When they arrived, Jerry was five and Gen was three. Lena, born in 1906, was named after Antonina and was very close to her grandmother who told her, "You can be poor but you don't need to be dirty. Keep yourself clean and your clothes clean."

Calogero lived seven, and Antonina twelve years in Geneseo, enjoying their grandchildren from the marriages of Nicolo and Fortunata and Giuseppa and Joseph Aprile. After Calogera died, Antonina moved in with her son Giovanni and his wife Agnes.

CHAPTER 23
Daily Life in Geneseo

Life in Geneseo during the first three decades of the twentieth century was filled with challenges. The winters were cold with heavy snows coming off Lake Ontario. Town staff had to keep sidewalks and roads clear using manpower and horse power. Large blocks of ice were harvested from the rivers and lakes and carried to the ice house on sleds pulled by horses.

During trips to the Birdseye-Snider canning factory at the bottom of Court Street near the Erie Train Depot, beans and corn would often fall off the heavily loaded trucks going down the steep hill. Boys on Court Street were quick to scoop up the droppings and take them home.

After the three varieties of grapes were harvested, Nicolo had to work on the town roads and infrastructure to prepare for the long winter. If the town decided to build a sidewalk, the crew would prepare the site using hand tools, then mix, pour and finish the concrete. If utilities and sewers were needed, the crew dug the trenches, placed the lines and did the necessary hookups. If a repeat project was needed, often Nicolo would be asked to direct the crew to the location of a particular utility. He had a photographic memory and could tell them the exact location to dig. After he retired from the Town of Geneseo, Nicolo was often consulted into his late sixties and early seventies, since his memory and past experience were of great value in planning and completing projects.

Nicolo had difficulty with English. With his brother Giuseppe's help, he was able to read and write enough to pass the examination for citizenship in June 1911. His daughters were especially good at speaking both Italian and English and were helpful to him and Fortunata in transacting family business.

Nicolo was active in St. Mary's Catholic Church, where he was an usher and helped maintain the building and grounds. Each Sunday, Nicolo would put on a suit and tie and his polished boots and walk the half mile up Court Street to Mass. Mary, his youngest daughter, started playing the organ and singing at St. Mary's as a teenager. His grandsons would often be altar boys when Nicolo ushered and Mary sang and played the organ. A number of his and Fortunata's relatives had migrated to Geneseo and attended St. Mary's.

Following Mass on Sunday, Nicolo and Fortunata would welcome friends and relatives into their home for food and wine. On warm summer days, they would set up tables in their yard and have picnics. These picnics were elaborate, with different entrees served over several hours. Sunday was a complete day of rest and a family day with no work permitted.

Nicolo was not called up to serve in World War I. He received a deferment because of his loss of smell, poor eyesight and his large family. His brother Giuseppe, also a U.S. citizen, did serve in the Army as a weapons instructor. He was a marksman and was comfortable with all types of weapons. Giuseppe was a linguist who could read, write and speak Latin, Italian and English. He lived alone on five acres of land on upper Court Street and continued to raise grapes on his land after the war ended.

Fortunata was a good mother who provided the best for her children. In addition to her business skills, she was noted for her ability to diagnose and treat various common injuries. Many of her neighbors and friends did not speak English and were not comfortable with American doctors. Fortunata was a natural healer. She instinctively knew how to care for those needing care. Even the physicians in the small town marveled at her ability. She listened attentively to the sick and was usually able to provide a remedy. She had very sensitive hands and could examine and feel the injured part and come up with a diagnosis. If there was a fracture, she would send the person off to Dr. Southall, the town doctor. If there was a contusion, strain or sprain she would undertake the treatment.

Fortunata had asthma which plagued her all her life. In her later years, she suffered a number of pulmonary attacks which ultimately led to her death in 1948.

CHAPTER 24

Trips to Geneseo

During World War II, there were no cars available to buy. All metal, even scrap, was collected for use in building ships, planes and armored vehicles. Just after the war, my dad, Joe Nasca, found a four-door 1938 Chevrolet car body. Over a period of six months, he found an engine, transmission and other necessary parts and rebuilt the car.

We were living in a row house in Anacostia in the southeast area of Washington, D.C. My mother, Lena Disparti Nasca, had not seen her father Nicolo and her mother Fortunata for five years.

In early August 1946, just after daybreak, Mom, Dad, Gerry and I made our first trip north to Geneseo in the black '38 Chevy. After many stops to check and add oil and water to the radiator, we arrived in Geneseo as the sun was setting.

We spent three weeks of Dad's vacation in Geneseo each year in August. Aunt Gen and Mary went out of their way to prepare our favorite foods, introduce us to their friends and store keepers in town, and provide trips and fun things to do.

We were treated to fresh vegetables from Nicolo's garden and learned to eat boiled stuffed artichokes and fava beans with pasta. Small glasses of grandfather's red wine mixed with Canada Dry ginger ale were provided to my sister and I around age twelve. After dinner, I would climb the Seckel pear tree in the front yard and harvest the small pears to eat. I quickly learned that too many of these small, grenade-shaped pears could keep you going to the bathroom most of the night.

One day, Nicolo, at my aunt's urging, asked me to pick lettuce from his garden for the dinner salad. When I returned, having picked several of the entire plants, Nicolo dressed me down in Sicilian, saying, "You are one damned hardheaded Calabrese."

There were a lot of kids our age on Court Street, so we kept busy each day playing with our new friends. Each week, Peter Bondi would take the neighborhood kids to Conesus Lake to teach us to swim. Even on the hot days of August, the lake water was very cold.

Every few days, Aunt Mary would play the organ or piano to accompany me on my violin. On the weekends, Carl Disparti would sing and play his trumpet. One Sunday afternoon, we were treated to Nicolo and Fortunata dancing the Tarantella, a popular Sicilian dance named after the poisonous tarantula. Over the next ten minutes, we saw very precise dance moves with a gradual increase in repetition as the tempo of the music accelerated.

About once a week, I would visit with Uncle Joe on upper Court Street where he would let me shoot one of his 22-gauge rifles. I became quite fond of Uncle Joe's Winchester 22 rifle. Uncle Joe started my older cousins and me on tin-can targets at twenty-five yards, placed in the open areas between the rows of grape vines. As we learned to sight the rifle and control breathing, he had us shoot at paper targets progressively placed further away until we were comfortable with targets at fifty yards. Once in a while we got to shoot at a groundhog because they made large ugly tunnels through the vineyards.

After much begging and with the intervention of my aunts, my mother finally agreed to let me take the Winchester 22 home to Bethesda. During free time in the summers, I would carry my gun in a leather case up to Wisconsin Avenue, a few blocks from my house, and hitch a ride to a large vacant lot five miles north to hunt small animals and target shoot on land that a few years later became the Congressional Shopping Center.

We made a few car trips to Geneseo at Christmas time. As we entered New York State, we encountered a fresh snowfall and enjoyed the brightly decorated homes covered in snow as we passed through Elmira, Corning, Painted Post, and Bath, New York.

We had a lot of fun at Christmas with my brother Ed, who was nine years younger. One year, Frank Ricotta, a cousin of my mother and the postmaster of Geneseo, came dressed as Santa Claus just as Ed was being readied for bed. Frank brought presents for Ed, who was overtaken with joy and wonder. A few years later, I was dressed up as Santa, but Ed smelled a rat and pulled off my beard.

CHAPTER 25

Nicolo Becomes Gravely Ill

Nicola was an avid fisherman. He was frequently seen on the Genesee River with his fishing tackle and several strings of fish which he shared with his family and friends. One hot day, he caught a string of fish and took them home. Fortunata and Aunt Mary did not eat the fish. Nicolo had them for supper that evening. A few weeks later he developed a fever and rash. He began to hallucinate due to high fevers. He was taken to his family doctor who took one look at him and had him transported to Strong Memorial Hospital in Rochester, New York, thirty-five miles east of Geneseo.

The doctors and house staff at Strong were perplexed with what was wrong with him. It was difficult for them to get much information out of him since he would not talk with them.

Gen and Mary were with him and tried to get him to eat the hospital food but he would have nothing to do with it. All he wanted to do was sleep and be left alone. He was given IV fluids and placed in isolation. After a few days, the chief of medicine, a first-generation Italian American, came to see him. He spoke to Nicolo in Italian and asked him about growing grapes. Nicolo's eyes brightened and he started to talk about growing grapes. The doctor asked him if he had eaten fish recently. He told him about the fish that he had caught in the Genesee River. That morning the chief had read a report of a case of typhoid fever from contaminated fish caught in the Genesee River near Rochester. Within a few hours they started Nicolo on antibiotics. A few days later he came out of his shell and started to eat and talk.

After two weeks at Strong Memorial Hospital, Gen and Mary took him back home to Geneseo. During his hospitalization he lost 30 pounds due to persistent diarrhea and starvation. After a month, he regained his strength and some weight, and got back to work in his vineyards.

CHAPTER 26

Fortunata Passes

After Fortunata died in 1948 from complications due to worsening asthma, she was taken to the Rector-Hicks Funeral Home. There, she was prepared and dressed to return to her home where she could be viewed by her friends and neighbors in an open casket for three days before she was buried at St. Mary's Catholic Cemetery in Geneseo.

After she died, Nicolo kept himself busy tending his vineyards. Uncle Giovanni had died and Nicolo now had seven acres of grapes to care for. They required pruning, row after row, using hand tools. The soil was somewhat sandy, mixed with brown to black clay. Due to adequate rainfall, irrigation was not needed. The vines were neatly trellised with heavy wire and staked with solid oak timbers at each end. Frequent soil tilling by hand and weeding were needed.

Nicolo would start to work in the vineyards after breakfast, return home at noon for his main meal of the day, then take a brief nap on his porch before returning to the vineyards at two o'clock. He worked his vineyards every day but Sunday.

Nicolo and stepbrother Rosolino on the front porch after lunch

During the fall harvest in mid-September, the Geneseo children were taken out of school to help with harvesting the grapes. The majority of the grapes were sold to the Taylor Wine Company in Hammondsport, New York. Grapes, not as robust, were sold to make Welch's grape juice.

The choicest grapes were kept for making Nicolo's red and white wines. He had his own wine press and with uncles Giovanni and Joe made several barrels of wine each year. The reds were very pleasant with no harshness or after taste. He preferred to serve the reds out of a decanter, cooled, but not cold. Later, because of an irritable stomach, Nicolo had to mix his red wine with ginger ale. Wine was always part of the dinner meal. His grandchildren were allowed to have small glasses of red wine which was mixed with ginger ale. His white wines were reserved for Sunday and special days. The whites were kept in special oak barrels in the earthen basement under his house.

Additional vines were planted on five acres of land owned by his brother Joseph on land east of his house on upper Court Street. The income from the grapes made the difference between just getting by on Nicolo's town salary and being able to provide a better life and environment for his young family. Unfortunately, none of his children or grandchildren took an interest in the vineyards. Several barrels of wine turned to vinegar after his death. The land was sold at a good profit to developers. When his grandson Richard and granddaughter Gerry visited Sicily and ate lunch at the Nasca Trattoria in Cerda, the red table wine tasted just like Nicolo's wine.

Nasca Trattoria in Cerda, Sicily

CHAPTER 27

Nicolo Comes to Bethesda

After Fortunata died, Nicolo faced long winters alone in the house on Court Street with his dog Blackie. Mary was away during the week teaching in Belmont, New York, but returned each weekend. Gen was working each day in Sonyea, New York, but came home each evening to prepare dinner for Nicolo.

Lena Nasca suggested that Nicolo come to Bethesda, Maryland, and spend the winter of 1952 with her, Joe, and her three children. The trip from Geneseo to Bethesda took about twelve hours by car in the 1950s, using Route 15 for most of the trip through Pennsylvania and Maryland. It was decided that Aunt Mary would drive Nicolo and his dog Blackie to Fry Brother's Turkey Ranch in Steam Valley, Pennsylvania, on Route 15. Dad and I would drive up from Bethesda and pick him up at Fry's.

Both cars arrived at the Turkey Ranch very close to one o'clock, so it was decided to go into the restaurant to have a turkey dinner. Blackie was left alone in Aunt Mary's car.

When we returned to the cars after eating our delicious turkey dinners, we found the lining from the interior roof of Aunt Mary's new Buick hanging down over the front and back seats. Aunt Mary was furious. Nicolo pulled Blackie out of the car and swatted him on the rear end with his walking stick. We quickly loaded grandfather's luggage into our car and waited for Nicolo and Blackie to get in to our blue-and-white 1951 Oldsmobile 88. which Dad had bought from his brother Al in Honeoye Falls, New York.

Nicolo was used to eating his main meal at noon, so my mother decided that I would come home from school each day at noon to join Nicolo for dinner. This meant getting permission to leave school and walk the half mile home for the noon meal. Although we had a small yard with some trees and bushes, Nicolo had nothing to do and was very bored. After five months we took him back to Geneseo with his dog Blackie. This was his last trip south.

CHAPTER 28
Nicolo Passes

Nicolo started having difficulty with passing urine in the spring of 1959. He was looking forward to pruning his grape vines and tilling the soil in anticipation of another harvest. April and May were cool and dry with ideal weather for working in the vineyards. However, Nicolo would tire and not be able to return to work after lunch. He gradually lost strength and would return home after an hour or two in the vineyards.

Gen and Mary took him to his local doctor and then to Strong Memorial, where they found him to have an enlarged prostate and probable prostate cancer at age 83. His kidneys were failing because of the enlarged cancerous prostate. He was not a candidate for surgery.

Gen and Mary brought him home and set up a hospital bed in the dining room where they cared for him. During his terminal illness, he had frequent visits by Dr. Southall and by several nurses from the Visiting Nurses Association, who changed his catheter and gave him medication for pain. He went into a coma a few weeks before he died on September 4, 1959.

After he died, he was laid out in an open casket for a few days before he was buried next to Fortunata at St. Mary's Cemetery in Geneseo.

CHAPTER 29

Court Street and Northview Houses

A few years after Nicolo died, the State of New York approached the residents on the west side of Court Street about purchasing their homes and land to make way for expansion of the Geneseo Normal School and the State University College of New York at Geneseo.

Gen and Mary Disparti agreed on the purchase of their home and land with the stipulation that their house be moved, rather than demolished, once the State purchased the land.

The house was lifted off its foundation and transported by truck to a lot purchased by Gen and Mary on Lower Court Street near the Genesee River. It was rented for a few years and later the house and land were sold.

37 Court Street house being transported by truck to Lower Court Street.

With the money they received from the sale of the Court Street house and from the sale of Nicolo's and Giuseppe's vineyards on Court Street, Gen and Mary built a modern two-story, three-bedroom house on Northview Drive.

The home was on a half-acre lot with a large area devoted to flower and vegetable gardens. These gardens produced numerous fresh vegetables and beautiful flowers during the summer months for all to enjoy. The bathrooms had heated floors. There was a large living room, dining area, library, a music room with a piano and organ, and a very modern kitchen on the first floor with a small bathroom. A large porch in the back of the house looked out over the gardens.

Nick Disparti's son, Gerry, told me that when he visited Aunt Gen in the late 1990s, he was driving a rental car and asked her, "Would it be okay if I park the rental car in the garage?" She told him it would be fine after he had the car washed.

On our visits to Geneseo, we always parked on the black macadam outside the garage for fear of doing damage to Aunt Mary's new Buick in the garage.

Our family spent many relaxing days during our summer trips to visit Gen and Mary in the Northview home. On most evenings, we would grill outside and eat on the back lawn with friends and relatives from Geneseo and Rochester.

CHAPTER 30
Genevieve Disparti

Genevieve Disparti was a gifted artist. She received a degree from the Rochester Institute of Technology in fine arts. She volunteered to serve with the Women's Army Corps during the Second World War. She was assigned to Camp Pine, a training site for General Patton's Fourth and Fifth Armored Divisions and the Forty-fifth Infantry in Fort Drum, New York.

Gen was responsible for planning and organizing social affairs and entertainment for the military stationed in the area. She was discharged in February 1944. During the war, she dated a war correspondent who asked her to marry him, but she turned him down.

During her deployment, she met Conrad Hilton, who was impressed with her organizational skills and offered to pay for her training in hotel management. She took him up on the offer and completed her training and worked for Hilton for a short time.

Gen was one of the first certified occupational thera-pists in the USA. She received her training at the Richmond Professional Institute of William and Mary College. Although she had several offers, she returned to Western New York as the Director of the Occupational and Manual Arts programs at Craig Colony for the disabled at Sonyea, New York. She worked at Craig until her retirement.

Aunt
Gen in
her WAC
uniform

After work each day, Gen would return home to
Geneseo and cook dinner for Nicolo. Each night before
going to bed around midnight, she would wash, dry, and
iron her gray occupational therapy uniform. She drove to
work each day in a top-of-the-line Buick that she kept only
three years before buying a new one.

Most of the patients at Craig were involved in farming,
animal care, auto repair and the manufacture of linens, rugs
and leather goods. They suffered from seizures, cerebral
palsy and other neurological diseases that prevented them
from living independently. The Craig community was most
beneficial to its residents and was self-sustaining.

Geraldine (Gerry) Nasca, Gen's niece, spent three
summers in the early 1960s at Sonyea as a student and

followed her aunt into the occupational therapy field, also completing her studies at the Richmond Professional Institute.

Gen Disparti, 1950

CHAPTER 31

Gen Disparti passes

After Gen retired from Craig Colony, she spent her time doing art and caring for her flower garden and home. One day, she developed a severe headache, became nauseated and collapsed on the couch in the living room. She was transported to Strong Memorial Hospital. When she arrived there, she was unresponsive and in a deep coma. She had suffered an intracerebral bleed due to a ruptured aneurysm within the brain tissue. It was not amenable to treatment. She died on Valentine's Day 1972 and was buried in St. Mary's Cemetery in Geneseo.

CHAPTER 32

Mary Disparti

Mary, the youngest of the Disparti children, was full of energy and her sister Lena was assigned to watch over her. One afternoon when it was getting close to dinner time, Lena found Mary at the school playground on the swings. Lena told Mary, "You need to come home for dinner."

But she kept swinging higher and higher. As she was descending, she fell to the ground and landed hard on her left side. She cried out, "I can't see out of my eye." She had dislocated the lens and had a detached retina of the left eye as result of the fall. At the time, there was no treatment.

In spite of her disability, she was an excellent student and learned to play the organ and drive a car as a teenager.

Mary Disparti graduated from the Geneseo State Normal School in 1931 with a degree in primary education. Her first teaching assignment was in a two-room school house in Varysburg, New York, where she taught grades one through eight for six years. She taught in Johnsburg, New York, for two years in another two-room school house.

In 1943, she was transferred to the Belmont Central School where she established a kindergarten class and taught first and second grades. Mary was an advocate for teaching math and science in the early grades and in using audiovisual aids in the classroom.

She was honored as the New York Grade School

Teacher- of- the- Year in 1974 on Mary Disparti Day in Belmont, New York. She retired after thirty-seven years of classroom teaching.

Mary Disparti, college graduation, and later in the 1950s

She was the principal organist at St. Mary's Catholic Church in Geneseo for fifty years. Genevieve and Mary cared for Nicolo and Fortunata in the Court Street house until they passed away. Mary enjoyed traveling and was fond of overseas tours with friends and family. She founded the Livingston County branch of "Young at Heart," a senior group that met on a regular basis to exchange information, socialize and volunteer for community projects. She was honored in 1986 as the Geneseo Citizen of the Year.

PARADE BEGINS — Holding the hand of one of her kin
dergarten children, Mary Disparti walks in a parade in he
honor in Belmont Wednesday. Miss Disparti, who has tar
in Belmont since 1943, was feted at a surprise party T'
Wednesday was declared Mary Disparti Day in Bel
(Reporter

Mary Disparti presiding over Young at Heart meeting

Mary frequently visited her nieces and nephews. When we visited her in Geneseo, she always had family and friends over to visit and enjoy evening cookouts, conversation and music. As she approached her final years, she was hospitalized for treatment of renal cancer at Strong Memorial. When she returned home, she was unable to live alone and was moved to the County Nursing Home where she died in 2002.

CHAPTER 33

Jerry Disparti Family

Jerry Disparti, Nicolo's son, worked in a shoe factory in Rochester. Just prior to the onset of World War II, he opened up a shoe repair business. He and his wife, Frances Giunta, had two sons, Nick and Carl. Because of recurrent bouts of bronchitis and asthma, Jerry Disparti sold his shoe repair business and moved to Chula Vista, California. He later moved to Escondido, California in the late 1950s to be close to his son Nick.

Jerry
Disparti,
age 18

Frances Giunta Disparti with Mary & Gen

Nick Disparti, after finishing Edison Technical School, had no plans to attend college. In spite of his parents' and Aunt Gen and Mary's pleadings to attend a vocational or technical college, he volunteered to serve in the Army Air Force during World War II. He was stationed in Germany during the end of the war as an aircraft mechanic.

While there, Nick spotted a beautiful, full-sized violin that was for sale. He spoke with the owner, who said he would sell the violin for 100 cartons of American ciga-rettes. Nick contacted my dad and let him know about the cost of the violin. I was playing a three-quarter sized violin and was ready to purchase a full-sized violin. Dad purchased fifty cartons of Camel and fifty cartons of Lucky Strike cigarettes and had them shipped to Nick. A few weeks later, the full-sized violin arrived at 1409 18th Place in Washington, D.C. Frank Jeziseck, my violin teacher and next-door neighbor, restrung the violin and tuned it prior to having me play it.

When Nick returned from service, he attended an industrial technical school in Buffalo, New York. There he met a fellow student, Frank Romeo, who introduced Nick to his sister and future wife, Val Romeo. They were married in Rochester, New York in 1951.

Nick graduated from the George Peabody Institute in Nashville, where he received his undergraduate degree in Industrial Arts, and from Long Beach State University for his master's degree.

Nick and Val moved to Escondido, California, where Nick began his 35-year career teaching industrial technology at Escondido High School and later directed the program at Palomar Community College.

Nick Disparti, 1987

Nick and Val had a girl, Julie, and two boys, Jerry and Stephen. Nick died in Escondido at age eighty-six, in 2012.

Carl Disparti joined the Air Force after he finished high school. He later obtained a degree in Business Administration from Loyola University in Baltimore, Maryland. He did sales and marketing for Minolta. He and his wife Geri had three children, Cathy, Nickie and Lois. Carl died in Venice, Florida in 2011.

Carol and Carl Disparti, 1987

Carl Disparti, Nick Disparti, Nick's son Jerry, Carl's wife Gere, Nick's daughter Julie, Nick's wife Val, Nick's son Steven; foreground: Carl's daughters Cathy and Lois and son Nickie

Nickie, Carl, Cathy Disparti, Lena Nasca, Gen Disparti, Gere and Lois Disparti

CHAPTER 34

The D'Aprile Family

Giacomo D'Aprile, born in January 1832 in Valledolmo, Sicily, and Fortunata Vollone, born in July 1841, were married in 1854. Fortunata was thirteen and was to have a child every year, sixteen children, between 1860 and 1885, eight of whom survived.

Giacomo D'Aprile and Fortunata Vallone's son Joseph, born in 1869, married Giuseppa Latona, my grandmother Fortunata Disparti's sister.

Gravestone of Giacomo Aprile, wife Fortunata Vollone Aprile and two deceased children.

Antonio (Tony) D'Aprile, their son, born in June 1870, married Catherine Miceli in Valledolmo in 1888 and they had six children. He was one of the first influential Sicilians to settle in Western New York state. He came to Buffalo, New York, in 1892 and worked as a tinsmith and plumber. A few years later he moved to Geneseo where Harold Doty made him the foreman at the Belden canning factory. He brought his parents, Giacomo and Fortunata, to Geneseo in 1893 with his sister Giuseppa, age eleven, and employed them in the canning factory.

Antonio D'Aprile

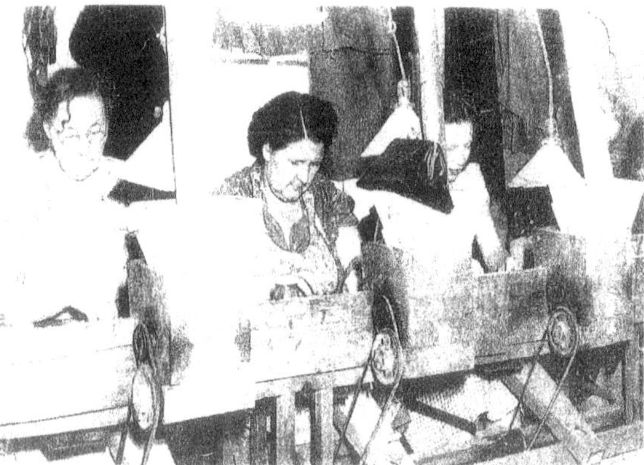

Women working sorting beans in the canning factory on lower Court Street, courtesy of "Court Street Community" booklet, 2012

He partnered with Tony Battaglia to open the M & B grill in Geneseo. He opened a bank on Main Street to make it easier for immigrants to get loans and buy land. Tony purchased a large tract of land on the north side of town, created small lots in and around Court Street and sold them to the new arrivals from Sicily. He often purchased their passage to New York, got them jobs and made sure they had at least 25 U.S. dollars when they entered the U.S. so the inspectors at Ellis Island would not turn them away as being destitute. The family operated a dry goods store in Geneseo, and Tony formed and directed the Aprile Royal Italian Band of Mount Morris, New York. The Aprile family donated the bell for St. Mary's Catholic Church. Although he had only a grade school education, Tony was a translator for his friends, being fluent and able to read and write English and was a naturalization sponsor for several of his family and friends.

Tony and Catherina moved to Rochester in 1925 and lived in a large house on Lake Avenue. In 1929 he opened the Rochester Cement Block Works on Jay Street, and later AM Gasoline and Oil, and ran an insurance agency. One wonders if Tony and Papa Nasca were friends since the Nasca grocery store was located at 332 Jay Street, a few blocks from Tony's Cement Block Works, also on Jay Street. Possibly, Papa Nasca filled up his trucks at Tony's nearby gas stations?

Michael DeFrancisco, grandfather of Joey Nasca and Michael Nasca Scarciotta, worked for Tony as a bookkeeper. One day when Michael was counting money, he was attacked and beaten around his head. He credited his sturdy derby hat for saving his life.

After his wife Catherina died in 1938, Tony returned to Geneseo. He died in March of 1952 in Rochester, still an active businessman operating a general insurance brokerage.

Joseph D'Aprile, Tony's brother, changed the family name to Aprile. He settled in Batavia, New York, and worked as a shoemaker. In August of 1900, he moved to 52 Court Street in Geneseo. Joseph and Giuseppa Latona Aprile had six children: Carrie in 1897, Charles in 1900, Frank in 1903, Antonio (Anthony) in 1904, Marie Antoinette in 1907 and Dominic in 1907.

Joseph and Josephine (Giuseppa) Aprile

Headstones of Josephine and Joseph Aprile

Riviera Theater, built by Joseph Aprile in 1914 in Geneseo, New York

Charles W. Aprile Sr., born in April 1900, served in the U.S. Army in the Medical Department with the Sixteenth Field Artillery in World War I and saw action in several battles in France.

Charles W. Aprile Sr., 1918, US Army Medical Department Sixteenth Field Artillery

He returned to Geneseo after the Armistice and in 1929 married Josephine Cipriano, born in Sicily in April 1908.

Josephine's father Charles Cipriano made her quit school after sixth grade to work in the family dry goods business in Mount Morris, New York.

Charles W. Aprile Sr. and Josephine Cipriano Wedding

Charles and Josephine ran the Riviera Theater (formerly the Rex) in Geneseo. The Riviera Theater was considered one of the finest and most complete playhouses in western New York, and was the go-to movie house until 1920 when the Grand Theater opened.

A few years later, Joseph Aprile bought out the Grand Theater and ran it until talking pictures brought a close to the Grand and a major renovation to the Riviera. Charles Aprile spent $8,000 to upgrade and lease the theater and showed the first picture with sound and motion ("cine-phone"), "Lucky Boy," starring George Jesse. Another first for the Riviera was the Sunday matinee, approved by a referendum taken by the Village of Geneseo allowing Sunday shows after two p.m. In November 1929, Charles Aprile renovated the theater by installing a pipe organ and increasing seating to 700. One wonders if Mary Disparti, Josephine's niece, was one of the first to perform on the new pipe organ?

The Riviera Theater was managed by Charles Aprile.

M.J. Kallet of Oneida and Sidney Kallet of Syracuse bought the Riviera and owned it for 20 years with Charles working as general manager. The Aprile family owned the theater building and were made independent operators of the theater in October of 1955.

Charles and Josephine had six children. Jacob was a gifted athlete and track star. He drowned in the Genesee River at age 17. Joseph, a graduate of Geneseo State

College and RIT, served for four years in the U.S. Air Force in Tokyo, Japan, as a mail censor during the Korean War. He married Takato, a Japanese woman, and lived in California until his death in 1994. Diane married Richard Camfield of Geneseo. Ronald and Robert, twin brothers, were born in 1939. Ronald ran the Geneseo liquor store and his brother Richard operated the Geneseo laundromat.

Charles W. Jr. (Chuck) was born in 1937 and went to "bank schools" in Maine and New Hampshire. He and James E. Wright opened Aprile Realty Corporation in Geneseo, and after several years as a broker, he became an officer at the Rochester Hanover Trust Bank. He and Joyce had two children, Dawn and Chip. Chuck died in March 2022.

Diane Aprile Camfield

Charles W. (Chuck) Aprile Jr.,
Oct. 31, 1936 to March 12, 2022

Ronald Aprile, Feb. 7, 1939
to Nov. 13, 2021

Robert (Benny) Aprile,
Feb. 7, 1939 to 1995

Laundromat owned and
operated by Robert Aprile,
1964-1992

Aprile Restaurant
around 1960,
6 Center Street,
Geneseo

Chuck Aprile and mother Josephine

PART II

CHAPTER 35

The Giuseppe Nasca Family

The Nasca family was from Cerda, Sicily. Cerda was inhabited by Spanish royalty in the sixteenth century. It was a popular resort town that became a yearly stop on the European car-racing circuit during the early twentieth century. The Targa Florio Classic drew race car drivers to the Sicilian coast each year to race up and down the steep hills and tight turns of former donkey tracks.

Nasca was a common family name in Cerda, which was located about twenty kilometers inland from the north coast of Sicily.

My paternal great-grandfather, Epifanio Nasca, was born in Cerda on January 11, 1832, to Carmelo and Rosa Faudale. He married Epifania Maggio, born in 1839. They had four sons: my paternal grandfather, Giuseppe, Papa Nasca, born September 30, 1865; Fernando, 1868; Ferdinando, 1872; Carmelo, 1877; and two daughters: Rosa, who died after birth in 1863; and Giuseppa, born in 1867. Epifanio ran a transport service, hauling coal, stones, farm goods and passengers.

Giuseppe Nasca's wife, Maria Epifania Gugliuzza, my paternal grandmother, was born in 1872 in Cerda. Her parents were Antonina Farraro and Loreto Gugliuzza, later changed to Galusha. They lived on Via Gugliuzza in a stone house. She was eighteen and Giuseppe twenty-four when they married in Cerda on January 5, 1890.

Nasca Family Tree

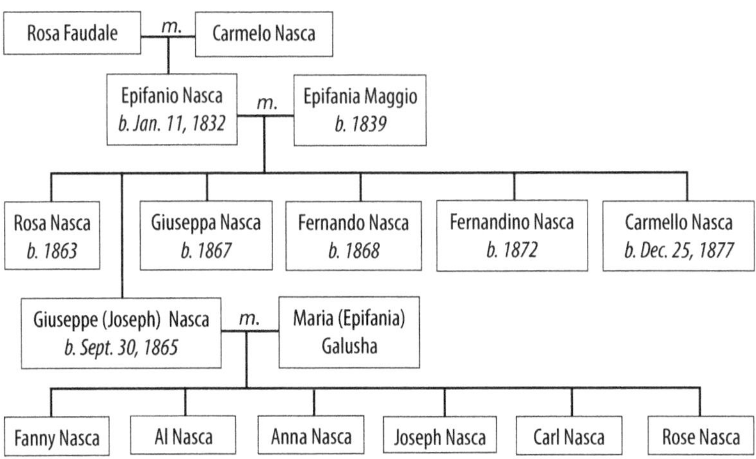

CHAPTER 36

Giuseppe's Life in Cerda

Giuseppe was baptized in the Church of the Assumption and attended the Catholic school of the Assumption in Cerda. He was a good student who excelled in running and soccer. He liked to ride horses. He was tall and very muscular with wide, broad shoulders and large ears.

After school, he would work in the family business, cleaning and fixing the transport wagons and carriages and tending the horses. On occasion, he would get to accompany one of the drivers on trips to Palermo or Marsala. After a few years, he had his own carriage and was licensed at age sixteen to be a transporter. His clientele appreciated his getting them to their destination on time.

One afternoon on his way to Palermo, his carriage was stopped by the Sicilian Mafia. There was no guard on the carriage. The passengers were terrified, but Giuseppe kept his cool.

One of the Mafia ruffians asked Giuseppe, "Are you transporting any bank money?"

Giuseppe replied, "There is no bank money."

The head mafioso said, "Get the passengers out, so we can search the carriage."

After they completed their search and found no money, they told Giuseppe, "Get the passengers back in the carriage and drive off. Tell no one of this holdup."

When he arrived in Palermo to discharge his passengers, they were met by the police who wanted to question him and his passengers about the holdup.

Giuseppe told them, "They searched my carriage, but found nothing and let us go."

This satisfied the police and they told him, "You are free to go back to Cerda."

After he had his lunch, he returned to his carriage. There was a family waiting near his transport that wanted a ride back to Cerda. He agreed to take them since he had no other clients. Anna and Loreto Gugliuzza had been shopping in Palermo for their daughters, Marie Epifania and Lucy.

CHAPTER 37

Giuseppe Meets Maria Epifania

A few days after transporting the Gugliuzzas back to Cerda, Giuseppe got a request from Loreto to take him and his daughter Marie Epifania to Palermo. She was interested in attending a girls' school to further her education. She was a very good student and wanted to be a teacher. She would attend the school run by the Sisters of Notre Dame, a French order of women who devoted their lives to teaching and ministering to the sick.

Giuseppe was impressed with fourteen-year-old Maria as she came out of her home to board the carriage with her father.

She said to him, "My father and mother have told me you are a very good driver and that you will get us safely to Palermo."

Giuseppe said he expected good travel conditions and a comfortable ride to Palermo. He said he would do his best to get her and her father safely to Palermo.

Loreto and Maria sat in the enclosed carriage with Giuseppe outside driving the team of two horses. After they arrived in Palermo at the girls' school, Loreto and Giuseppe had an espresso while Maria completed her interview.

Loreto was a successful businessman who traded in spices. He had five sons and two daughters.

He asked Giuseppe, "Do you plan to continue to be a carriage driver?"

Giuseppe said he had an interest in going to America "where the streets were paved in gold."

Loreto said he had heard that the Sicilian government was going to annex more land and businesses and the owners would need to pay taxes to use their land and keep their businesses.

Giuseppe told him that he and his family were very concerned about a future government takeover and the frequent Mafia raids on their transport service to and from Cerda to Palermo.

The Nasca family had considered hiring armed guards to accompany their carriages on trips to Palermo but could not afford to pay them and make money on the trips. They discussed stopping long distance trips and just doing local trips within Cerda.

After Maria finished her interview and tour of the school, her father met with the Sister Superior and paid her for Marie's first year of school which would begin in the fall. The return trip to Cerda was uneventful.

When they arrived in Cerda, Giuseppe asked Loreto, "Would it be possible for me to see Maria?"

Loreto said he would discuss that request with her mother, Antonina, and let him know when he could come to the house to see Maria.

Loreto paid Giuseppe and gave him a nice tip as they exited the carriage to their home on Via Gugliuzza.

A stone house
on
 Via Gugliuzza

CHAPTER 38

Giuseppe Nasca is Drafted

All able-bodied males in Sicily had to do military service. Giuseppe was examined and tested and was found to be fit for service in the Army. He was assigned to the cavalry in the Royal Sicilian Army. He turned eighteen just as the three-year Sicilian War against Britain and Italy was winding down in March 1883.

Sicily in the early 1800s wanted to modernize. Factories were being built all over the country. The government considered industrial progress important and diverted money from the military to be used for developing industrial capability. This proved to be a big mistake. If the North German Federation had not supported Sicily, the country would have lost the Battle of Naples and would have been occupied by Italian and British troops.

The Sicilian War was fought initially over control of the Sicilian region of Apulia. The United Kingdom wanted exclusive trading rights with Sicily. Forfeiture of these trading rights would destroy the Sicilian economy, as tariffs were one of Sicily's main sources of income.

Sicily saw this war as vital to keeping its independence. Sicily's key allies, the North German Federation, Russia and Austria, all declared war on Italy and the United Kingdom.

In the battle of Naples, Sicily lost 41,000 troops.

Russia, Austria, and the North German Federation stormed into Italy and fully occupied it. The war reached its end after a successful battle in the south of England where the North German Federation achieved a hard-fought victory.

At the time of the war, the Royal Sicilian Army and the Royal Sicilian Navy outnumbered the Italian Navy. Sicily also had carved out an empire in the Mediterranean while Italy was a newly reorganized country. Italy turned to all their European allies, but the only one to help them was Britain. Sicily remained unoccupied by Italian forces because troops from the North German Federation defeated the Italians invading Sicily. This secured the Sicilian homeland. Sicily also moved all of their Naval fleet to the Straits of Gibraltar to prevent British forces from reaching Sicilian territory. Italy ended up fully occupied by German, Austrian, and Russian forces. Despite all this, Britain did not surrender because of demands made by the Russian Empire and the North German Federation. These three allied forces crossed the Straits of Dover to occupy British provinces. The war ended in a disastrous defeat for Italy and the United Kingdom. With the collapse of Italy's power, it left Sicily a recognized great power. This victory also stopped British attempts at gaining influence over Sicily and getting exclusive trade rights.

After completing his compulsory service in the army, Giuseppe returned home to Cerda to manage the Nasca Transport Service. During his time in the Army, he was assigned to work in troop transport and learned a lot about organization and management. He hired some of his Army buddies to join him in his transport business. This enabled him to have a driver and an armed guard on each long-distance trip. His carriages were all upgraded to enclosed vehicles.

However, after a few years, the government imposed heavy tariffs on transport services and established weigh stations that charged fees based on the weight of the goods being transported. With diminishing revenues, Giuseppe found it difficult to pay his former Army friends and stopped having armed guards on most of the trips. The lack of security opened the door for frequent Mafia raids on his wagons and carriages.

CHAPTER 39

Carmelo Nasca is Shot

Carmelo was twelve years younger than his brother Giuseppe. He grew up in Cerda and was a good student. He was interested in a military career, so he applied and was accepted into the Sicilian Royal Military College, located in the former Jesuit college (The Nunziatella) in Pizzofalcone.

He completed his studies with high honors and was assigned to the infantry. He served with distinction and after a few years was promoted to captain in the Sicilian Army. He was a knowledgeable leader and respected by those under his command.

While leading his troops in a training exercise, he was accidently shot by one of his soldiers. He was taken to the Military Hospital in Palermo, where he was treated for a gunshot wound to his chest. He improved initially but later developed an infection that progressed and ultimately led to his death. The Nasca family requested that Carmelo be interred in Cerda. He was buried with full military honors alongside his deceased relatives.

CHAPTER 40

Giuseppe Marries
Maria Epifania Galusha

Giuseppe Nasca and Maria Epifania were married in the Municipality of Cerda on January 5, 1890 by the Mayor and Civil Service Officer, Calogero Russo di Antonio.

Lucy, Maria's sister, emigrated to America in 1898 and married Ignacio Congelosi, a construction laborer in Rochester, New York. They encouraged Giuseppe and Maria to come to America. Ignacio was listed as Giuseppe's contact person on his Ellis Island immigration papers.

Papa Nasca left Naples on the ship Tartar Prince bound for Ellis Island. He arrived in New York on May 9, 1899 at the age of thirty-three, with twenty dollars. He was on a contract to work in the coal mines in Pittston, Pennsylvania.

Steamship Trojan Prince which carried Italian and Sicilian immigrants from Naples and Genoa to Ellis Island during the late 1800s and early 1900s

Maria and her nine-year-old daughter, Fanny, came to America in January 1900 on the ship Sempione out of Naples to join Papa Nasca in Pittston. Life was difficult. The family lived in an apartment on Brown Street. Each day, Papa Nasca would get up early to go to work in the mines, leaving Maria and Fanny alone until he returned late in the day. Maria decided to keep herself busy by managing a boarding house for miners in Pittston.

Lucy, Maria's sister, invited Maria and Fanny to come to Rochester for a visit. After a few days in Rochester, Maria did not want to return to Pittston. However, she had a commitment to run the boarding house, and she reluctantly returned to the apartment on Brown Street.

She told Papa Nasca, "There is a large population of Sicilians in Rochester and there is a store with apartments for sale near the car barn in downtown Rochester. That would be a good location for a grocery store."

Papa Nasca did not like working in the coal mines and decided to move to Rochester as soon as his contract with the coal mine was completed. The Nascas lived with Lucy and her husband Ignacio until Papa Nasca had enough money to buy the future grocery store and apartments on the corner of Jay and Grape Streets.

There were six Nasca children born to Maria Epifania and Papa Nasca: Fanny was born in Cerda in 1890. Born at home at 332 Jay Street, Rochester, were Epifanio (Al), 1901; Anna, 1906; Joseph A., 1907; Carmelo (Carl), 1909; and Rose, 1911. The family lived in the apartments behind the store.

CHAPTER 41

The Store on Jay Street

Papa Nasca's store was a gathering place for young immigrants. They would use the store's address, 332 Jay Street, for mail delivery. He would hold their mail until they were able to pick it up. He also extended credit to newly-arrived families as well as to the Mafia. The Black Hand, the Mafia symbol, was displayed on the wall of the store indicating it was a place for the Mafia to trade.

Papa Nasca had three ledgers to record his sales. One was for people who paid cash, another for those on credit, and one for the Mafia. He used a code rather than their actual names to record the Mafia transactions.

Al Nasca, Papa Nasca and Carl Nasca in the Jay Street Grocery Store.

Papa Nasca got letters from the Mafia requesting he drop off 200 dollars at a local bank in a sealed envelope. Instead of money, he cut a newspaper up to the size of bills and placed them in an envelope which was dropped off at the bank. A few days later, a young man who came to the store frequently asked him, "Have you received any recent letters from the Black Hand?"

Papa Nasca told him, "No, I have not, because you have stopped sending them."

In addition to selling groceries, the store had a meat market next door until Papa Nasca had to fire the butcher, who was incompetent. Fanny Margo's husband, Louie, a shoemaker by day, opened an ice cream parlor at the store. The store also provided an American Express money order service.

Maria was even-tempered. She had her hands full raising the three boys, Al, Joe and Carl and the two girls, Anna and Rose. She had some help from her daughter Fanny until Fanny's children, John, Joe, Rose and Mary were born. Maria Epifania died of pneumonia at age 50.

Papa Nasca was a tall, imposing man with distinct facial features and large broad shoulders. He was very fair and did not have the skin color of a Sicilian. He got up early in the morning and retired late at night. In his sixties, he would run four-block races with the younger men in the neighborhood and often win. Because of his unusual facial features, he was chosen as a portrait model by the Rochester Art Club.

CHAPTER 42
The Banana and Beer Routes

Papa Nasca sold bananas to stores and fruit stands in Rochester. He would buy a train-car load of green bananas and bring them to the Jay Street store for "gassing."

He and his sons would carry the bananas on poles to the basement where he had built an enclosure with large hooks to support the weight of the banana trees. Most of the bananas he sold came from Central America and took nine months to grow before they were harvested in a green unripe state.

In order to ripen them, Papa Nasca used a mixture of ethylene and nitrogen to turn the bananas into a nice yellow color. The mixture of ethylene and nitrogen displaced oxygen out of the air during the gassing. After turning on the gas, the operator had to quickly get out of the enclosure for fear of suffocation.

Another concern was the presence of tarantulas hiding in the banana trees. The gassing was very effective in getting rid of them.

After the gassing, the Nasca boys would retrieve the ripened bananas, box them, and load them in the truck for Papa Nasca to sell on his banana route. They sold bananas and other fruits and vegetables on wooden stands in the front of the store on Jay Street.

Papa Nasca would buy several large kegs of beer from local breweries and deliver them to stores and bars in nearby towns, until Probation prevented the sale of alcoholic beverages in the late 1920s.

CHAPTER 43

Supply Truck Robbery

Papa Nasca would go to the central market at two in the morning to pick up produce and meats for his grocery store. One morning, with his truck full of goods, he was stopped by the Mafia and told, "Get out of the truck and leave the keys in."

A few minutes later, one of the bandits drove off with his truck full of goods. He walked back to the store several blocks away and arrived there at five a.m. He reported the robbery and his stolen truck to the police.

Later that day, a man came into the store asking for the owner. Carl was in the store and went to get his father, who was in the apartment.

The man asked him, "Was your truck stopped this morning and driven off full of your supplies?"

Papa Nasca said, "Yes, I was stopped around three this morning with my truck full and told to get out of the truck and leave the keys in."

The man then showed him his badge and told him he was a detective assigned to investigate the robbery.

The detective told him, "We want you to take a truck to the market tomorrow at two in the morning and load it up with your supplies. We will have two men in the back of the truck with guns to accompany you back to the store.

"If you are stopped by the Mafia, do as they say and get out of the truck and run away.

"Our men will come out of the back of the truck and apprehend the bandits."

The next morning, Papa Nasca loaded up his truck at central market with two armed men in the back and drove off as instructed by the detective. He drove to the store without being stopped. When he arrived at the store, one of the two armed men said, "Let us know when you are going to the market again and we will meet you there."

The following week, Papa Nasca drove to the market and loaded up his supplies for the trip back to the store. Two men got in the back of the truck as before and he drove off.

As he was nearing his store on Jay Street, a car overtook him with men pointing guns out of the windows of a black sedan. He immediately pulled over and stopped the truck.

Again, he was told, "Get out and leave the keys in the truck."

He got out of the truck and ran to a corner store for cover as the men in the back of the truck came out and exchanged gunfire with the men in the black sedan. Within a few minutes, police cars pulled up to assist the two detectives. Two of the four bandits were killed and the other two were wounded and taken into custody.

CHAPTER 44
Name Change

When Joseph "Papa" Nasca came to the United States to work in the coal mines in Pittston, Pennsylvania, his last name was spelled Naska on the forms and identification papers he was given at Ellis Island.

His store signs, advertising, and the children's birth certificates all had Naska as the spelling of their names.

When Joseph A., my dad, was in high school, although he spoke Sicilian, he elected to take Italian. After a few weeks in class, he asked his teacher, "Why does the Italian language not have a 'k' in its alphabet?" His teacher told him there was no 'k' in the Italian language and that his name was misspelled.

He proceeded to tell Papa Nasca that the Naska name was misspelled. Papa Nasca, realizing that he would need to spend a great deal of money to redo signs, advertisements and birth certificates, told Joseph A., "Son, you'd better talk to the head Italian professor at the University of Rochester and have him write out on a piece of paper how our name is to be spelled in English."

A few days later, Joseph A. made an appointment to see the professor of Italian at the University of Rochester. He was told again, "Your name is misspelled. There is no 'k' in Italian." The professor wrote out NASCA on a piece of paper that he gave to Joseph A. to give to his father.

Papa Nasca, after seeing the paper from the professor, went ahead and had the storefront signs changed, all the interior signage redone, and the birth certificates of his six children corrected to the proper spelling, Nasca.

One wonders what would have happened to our last name if my dad had not decided to study Italian.

Photo taken around 1911 in front of the Nasca store on the corner of Grape and Jay Street in Rochester. An unknown person penciled in the names of the people in the picture: Uncle Jimmy? Gugliuzza, Papa Nasca with Al Nasca, Maria holding Carl Nasca, Vincenza holding Ross, Rose Magro? and Anna Nasca sitting on steps, Steve Magro holding John Magro?, two unknown men standing on the stairs, Tony Conigifi and Mr. Celentano standing on the street.

There was a bell on the door in the store that would ring each time a customer came in. Usually Maria, Fanny or Anna would come over to wait on customers since Papa Nasca was out selling bananas and delivering beer on his routes.

Papa Nasca in his
new Buick

CHAPTER 45

Tough Years

After Maria died of pneumonia in 1922, Papa Nasca was emotionally down and financially on his back. Maria had purchased a $1,000 life insurance policy that brought much-needed money to the family after her death. With five children to feed and clothe, Papa Nasca struggled to keep the family together, run the store and continue to service his banana and beer routes in the years following Maria's death.

High stock prices, out of sync with production and consumer demand for goods, caused a market bubble that burst on October 24, 1929—the famous "Black Thursday" stock market crash.

The most visible effects included widespread unemployment, homelessness, and a marked decrease in Americans' standard of living. In addition, a severe drought produced the Dust Bowls, a series of damaging dust storms. This environmental disaster ruined many farmers during a period when the economy was largely agricultural.

President Herbert Hoover (1929–1933) did nothing to stop the free fall of the American economy. His successor, Franklin Delano Roosevelt, elected president in a landslide victory in 1933, acted quickly to create jobs and stimulate the economy through the creation of "a New Deal for the forgotten man"—a program for people without resources to support themselves or their families. The New Deal was formalized as the federal Works Progress Administration (WPA), an umbrella agency for the many programs created to help Americans during the Depression, including infrastructure projects, jobs programs, and social services.

After Al finished high school, he spent more time helping Papa Nasca manage the store. Joseph A., Carl, Anna and Rose also helped after school and during their summer vacations.

Al and Carl, with other investors, bought a candy factory in 1928. Space was needed to store candy and gum products for distribution to stores and vending machines. At Al's suggestion, Papa Nasca agreed to provide storage space in the store for the candy factory's products. Later, Al converted the grocery store into a candy and tobacco store.

Fanny, Al and Anna married and moved out of the Jay Street apartments. Joseph A. was working for AT&T and taking night classes so he was rarely available to work in the store. Al was busy with the candy factory and Carl was working for the City of Rochester in addition to helping Al with distribution of the candy factory products. Rose was left to help Papa Nasca run the Jay Street candy store, until he left for Elmira to live with Joseph A. in 1938.

CHAPTER 46

Fanny Nasca and Louie Magro

Fanny Nasca, the oldest Nasca child, was a gregarious, attractive teenager who had a quick mind and was good at math. She was efficient and accurate in adding up prices and writing out bills for items purchased and recording them in the proper ledger. She enjoyed meeting and helping the customers.

Luigi (Louie) Magro, born in 1881, came to California from Agrigento, Sicily, at the age of nineteen to work on the railroad. His father was Giovanni Magro and his mother's maiden name was Celentano. He had two brothers and a sister, Geraldine. His older brother Steve came to Rochester from California. After a few years of working on the railroad, Louie got a job in Rochester working for the John Kelly Shoe Factory. He was always well-dressed in a suit and tie with a lapel handkerchief when he came to the store to pick up his mail.

One day while picking up his mail, he told Fanny, "I make gelato and ice cream. Would your father be interested in opening an ice cream parlor in the store?"

Papa Nasca told Fanny. "Tell Louie that I am interested in talking with him about doing an ice cream concession in my store."

A few days later, Louie came in to pick up his mail, and Papa Nasca was there in the store.

He came over to Louie and asked him, "What do you have in mind?" Louie told him his family in Agrigento made ice cream and gelato and that he wanted to do the same in Rochester, but he did not have the money to open a store.

Papa Nasca liked the well-dressed, mild-mannered young man and invited him to join him for a glass of wine. After a few glasses of wine, it was decided to give the ice cream concession a try. Fanny was to work out the details with Louie.

Fanny told Louie, "You can use our kitchen to make the ice cream and gelato, but you will need to buy the milk and other ingredients from our store, and give the Nascas 50 percent of the sales revenue."

Louie agreed to the terms and a few days later after finishing his work at the shoe factory came over to make ice cream and gelato in the Nasca kitchen. A week later, he opened his ice cream and gelato business, which was a great addition to the store services and well-received by the local clientele.

A few months later, Louie approached Papa Nasca and said, "I like Fanny, and may I have your permission to ask her to marry me?"

Papa Nasca told Louie," She is a young girl of fifteen and you are much older. She has a mind of her own. Don't be disappointed if she turns you down, but you have my permission to ask her."

Fanny and Louie eloped in 1906. A short time after that, they went back to Rome to obtain a blessing of their marriage. After they returned with their blessed marriage, they lived in one of the apartments connected to the store.

Fanny had finished school and worked full time in the store until John was born in 1907, followed by Joe in 1909, Rose in 1912 and Mary in 1914. John and Joe Magro were about the same ages as their cousins Al and Joseph A. Nasca, and they often played together in the backyard of the store.

Fanny
Nasca
Magro
and Luigi
Magro

Fanny, Mary,
Rose and
Louie Magro

Fanny Nasca on her wedding day with her mother, Maria Epifania

Galusha-Nasca-Magro Family Tree

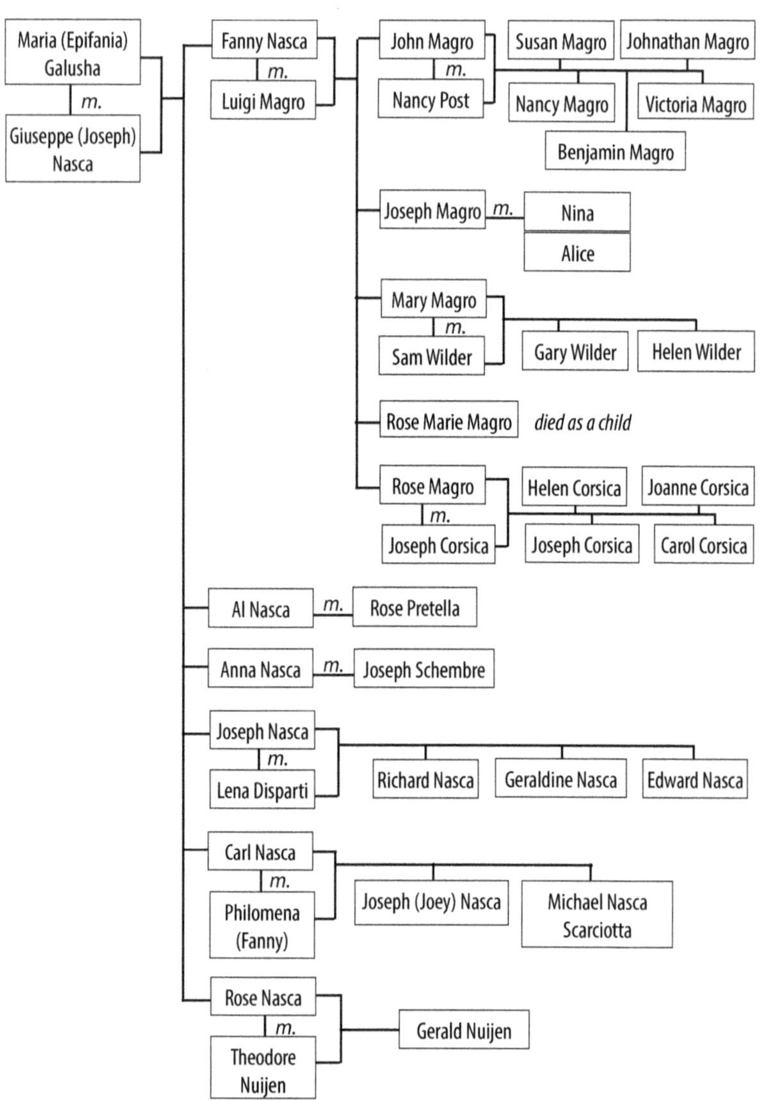

CHAPTER 47

John Magro Family

John Magro was born on September 15, 1907. After completing high school in Rochester, New York, he graduated from Harvard University with a degree in philosophy in 1932. He married Nancy Post, born December 4, 1919. Nancy was the first grandchild of Charles Dana and Irene Langhorne Gibson and the grand-niece of Lady Nancy Astor, the first woman to become a British Member of Parliament. John and Nancy were married in 1943 at St. James Episcopal Church in New York City.

John was a successful businessman who served on the board of trustees of the Cincinnati Opera for twenty-one years. He died April 18, 1998. Nancy died April 7, 2003. John and Nancy were married for fifty-five years and had five children: The Rev. Susan M. Pfeil, born February 28, 1945; Jonathan Magro, February 5, 1947 to July 24, 2017; Nancy L. Magro, born January 22, 1949; Victoria Magro Pfeil, Ph.D., October 31,1950 to December 19, 2000; and Benjamin Magro, born February 27,1952.

The family lived at Markin Farm in Montgomery, Ohio. Nancy and the family ran a riding stable. John would bring the children to Rochester on the Greyhound bus to visit with Fanny and Louie. The children had a deep love for Grandma and Grandpa Magro who always welcomed them with open arms when John brought them, all the way from Montgomery to Rochester. The family were regular attendees at the Cincinnati Summer Opera, The Cincinnati Symphony Orchestra concerts, The May Festival, and the ballet.

Ben, Mother Nancy and John, seated; Nancy and Victoria facing parents at sides of chair; Susan and Jonathan in the back.

Front: Benjamin, Nancy, Victoria. Back: Susan, Mom Nancy, and Jonathan

John and Nancy Magro

Nancy Magro

John Magro

Markin Farm,
Montgomery,
Ohio

CHAPTER 48
Joe Magro

Joe Magro graduated from the Rochester Institute of Technology and married Nina, his high school sweetheart. He was an artist with Disney in California and drew many of the original Disney characters. Later, he opened his own advertising business in Florence, Italy. He did many illustrations for Coca-Cola and other American companies.

Joe Magro

Louie, Fanny Joe
and Mary Alice
Magro

CHAPTER 49

Mary Magro Wilder

Mary Magro graduated from Rochester Institute of Technology with a degree in dietetics. She moved to New York City and worked as a dietician for the YMCA. She was hit by a car driven by a drunk driver while crossing a street near the YMCA and suffered a fractured leg.

She moved to Washington, DC, and met Sam Wilder in 1942. She worked as the first dietician for the Marriott's Airport Food service on US Route 1 in Virginia. Her job was to supervise the meals prepared by Marriot for National Airlines. Sam and his brothers, Zeke and Fletcher from Clayton, North Carolina, were also working at the National Airport with Marriott's Airport Food Service.

Sam and Mary Wilder had two children, Gary and Helen. Gary succumbed to multiple inoperable brain tumors. Helen became a radiology technician after graduating from Averett College. She married Clyde Gibson Jr. and they had two children, Amy and Clyde III.

Mary Magro
and
Anna Nasca

Gary and Sam Wilder

Helen and Mary Wilder

Helen Gibson, Clyde Jr., Mary Magro Wilder, Clyde Gibson Sr. and
Amy Gibson

CHAPTER 50

Rose Magro Corsica

Rose Magro and Joseph Corsica, 1934

Rose Magro, born November 19, 1912, married Joseph Corsica, born April 12, 1903, in 1934. Rose had a master's degree in education from University of Rochester and did special education. Joe had a master's in sociology and was a parole officer and social worker. He taught at Roberts Wesleyan College. Joe died in 1969 and Rose in 1996.

Helen Corsica, born April 28, 1935, was afflicted with celiac disease.

Joe Corsica Jr., born January 30, 1937, had a Ph.D. in counseling and psychology and a master's in social work. He taught at State University of New York (SUNY) Brockport. He died in February 2020.

Joanne Corsica, born April 3, 1942 had a master's in linguistics and PhD in social and cultural anthropology. She taught at State University of New York (SUNY) Empire

State College. She and her husband, Maris, live
in Rochester.

Carol Corsica Dzenis, born May 4, 1945, and her
husband Karlis own a home-building construction company.

Karlis Dzenis (Carol Corsica's husband), Helen Corsica, Fanny Magro,
Rose Corsica, Joe Corsica Jr. with bride Judy, Joe Corsica Sr., and
Joanne Corsica

Helen Corsica, Joanne Corsica, Joe Corsica Jr., Maris Dzenis
(Joanne's husband) and Rose Corsica, sorting out Joanne's and Maris
wedding gifts

CHAPTER 51
Al Nasca

Al married Rose Pretella from Livonia, New York in 1926 and lived in one of the Jay Street apartments. Later, Al and his brother Carl with others purchased a factory that made candy and gum products for candy vending machines. After seventeen years, the other investors pulled their support, leaving Al and Carl to face the creditors.

Al purchased an Oldsmobile dealership and gas station and moved to Honeoye Falls, New York, after the war ended. A few years later, he and Rose settled in Alhambra, California. Al developed a very successful business selling Mexican food and spices to stores and restaurants from Los Angeles to the U.S.-Mexican border. He and Rose were married for over fifty years and had no children.

Al Nasca and Rose Pretella Nasca with best man & maid of honor

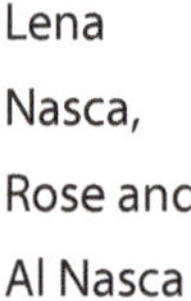

Lena
Nasca,
Rose and
Al Nasca

CHAPTER 52

Anna Nasca

Anna Nasca married Joseph Schembre in 1922. Joe was fifteen years older than Anna. She and Joe were planning on going for a picnic with friends on July 24, 1923. When Joseph came home to pick her up, he could not find Anna. As he stepped out into the hall to look for her, the door of a closet flew open and Anna fell at his feet with a revolver clutched in her right hand and a self-inflicted bullet wound in her right temple.

In a note she left, she said, "Dear Joe, I think I've tried to do my best. So please forgive me. Goodbye, Anna."

The family had planned to bury her next to her mother Maria in Holy Sepulcher Catholic Cemetery. However, the parish priest would not agree to bury her in the Catholic Cemetery since she had taken her own life. Because of the priest's decision, Papa Nasca wanted nothing more to do with the Catholic faith and he and his family stopped going to church. Anna was buried at Mount Hope Cemetery in Rochester.

Rose Magro,
Anna Nasca,
Mary Magro

CHAPTER 53
Joseph A. Nasca

While at West High school in Rochester, Joseph A. Nasca studied Latin, Italian, French, English and math. He planned to pursue a career in medicine. However, he responded to a recruitment ad from the American Telephone and Telegraph Company (AT&T) in his senior year at West High in 1927. They were looking for young men to train as lineman. He received six months' training in Buffalo, then returned to work in the recently opened Rochester office of AT&T, working on the K carrier transmission lines. Even though he had a full-time job, he continued to take evening college courses at the University of Rochester. He did not give up the possibility of pursuing a medical career. He worked in the Rochester office for ten years. He married Lena Disparti in August of 1937.

Joseph A. Nasca in canoe, 1930s

Joseph A. in
high school.
Note the
spelling of Naska
with a k.

CHAPTER 54

Carl Nasca Family

Carl was a plumber and also worked for the City of Rochester. He and his wife, Philomena (Fanny), had a son, Joseph (Joey), born in 1937, and they lived in a nice house on Woodstock Road in North Rochester.

Carl Nasca and Philomena (Fanny)

Michael was born in 1942. Fanny died eighteen months later. Joey went to live with Al Nasca and his wife Rose. Michael was adopted by his mother's sister, Madeline Scarciotta. Carl married Grace Provenzano in 1945.

Grace had a daughter, Phyllis. Grace and Carl moved back to Jay Street and Carl renovated the former store into additional living area and added apartments to rent out as a source of income.

The Nasca Grocery Store on the conner of Jay and Grape Streets in Rochester, NY, modified into apartments in 1950s

After his tour in the Army, Joey Nasca obtained boiler-maker and refrigeration licenses. He and Frances DeFrank married in 1961 and had two sons, Joseph and Michael. Joey worked for Xerox maintaining the plant's heating and air conditioning units until his diabetes caused him to lose his eyesight. He died in 1988 from a heart attack.

Michael Scarciotta graduated from Drake College in Fort Lauderdale in 1966 with a BBA. Michael was an insurance investigator for three years in Rochester and worked for thirty years with the city of St. Petersburg, Florida as a license inspector. He has a son, Brian Scott McCurdy, who lives in Washington, DC.

Carl Nasca with son Joey

Joseph (Joey) Nasca and brother Michael Scarciotta

Joseph and Frances DeFrank Nasca's wedding, June 1961

Michael Nasca, Joe Nasca Jr., Fran and Joey Nasca

Mr. and Mrs. Dominick DeFrank, Frances Nasca, Joe Nasca Jr., Rose Nasca Nuijen, Joey Nasca, Lena Nasca, Joseph A. Nasca and Michael Nasca

The Three Joes: Joe Nasca Jr., Joseph A. Nasca and Joey Nasca, 1987

CHAPTER 55

Rose Mary Nasca Family

Rose Nasca and Ted Nuijen
in 1942

Rose Mary Nasca, the youngest child, lived in an apartment on Jay Street and worked at the store until 1942 when she went to Washington, DC, to work for the government. She lived with her brother Joseph A. and his wife Lena. She met Theodore Nuijen, born in the Netherlands, in San Francisco. They were married in San Francisco in 1944. Their son, Gerald (Jerry), was born in 1945. Rose returned to Jay Street with her husband and Jerry in 1945 to help run the store but left two years later and returned to San Francisco. Jerry recalls that his father, who was a master carpenter, built a camper enclosure on the back of a truck to transport the family and their belongings back to San Francisco. Jerry was a schoolteacher and lives in Mill Valley, California, with his wife Inga. Rose died in 2002 in Nipomo, California.

Rose with son, Jerry, on her eightieth birthday

CHAPTER 56

The Galusha Family

Maria Epifania had six siblings: Frank, Lucy, Dominic, Jimmy, Rosolino (Russell Williams) and Nunzio. The Gugliuzza name was changed to Galusha.

Frank Galusha and his wife Camella had two boys, Joseph and Sam, and with his second wife Mary he had five children: Rose Amato, Josephine, Loretta, Rose and Larry.

Lucy Galusha was born February 12, 1890. She came to Rochester, New York in 1898. She married Ignacio Congelosi and moved to her home on Anthony Street in Rochester in 1910. Lucy and Ignacio had two daughters, Josephine and Annette. Josephine married Pasquale (Pat) Penna and they had three children: Teresa, Richard and Patricia. Annette married George Kuchala.

Dominic was a baker who lived in Geneva, New York. He and his wife Carnelia had five children: Kitty, Larry, Rose May, Dominic and Josephine. He was "fond of the drink." Later in life, he met Ethel, who worked in his restaurant as a waitress, and she got him to stop drinking.

Jimmy married Lilian and they had two daughters, Anna and Dorothy. He lived in Geneva and died of ALS in the 1940s.

Rosolino Galusha changed his name to Russell Williams. He settled in Pittston, Pennsylvania and purchased a tobacco and candy store over an inactive coal mine in downtown Pittston. He was married to Rosena. They had no children.

Nunzio married Antoinette. They had no children.

Galusha Family Tree

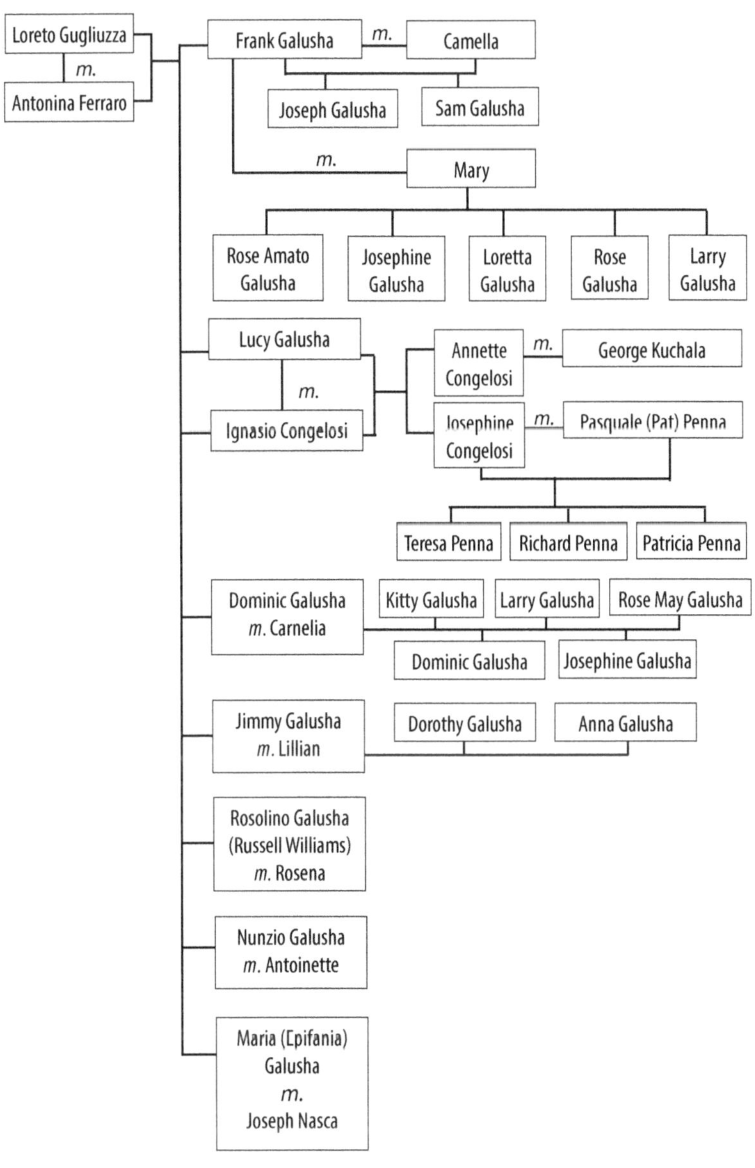

Galusha-Nasca-Magro Family Tree

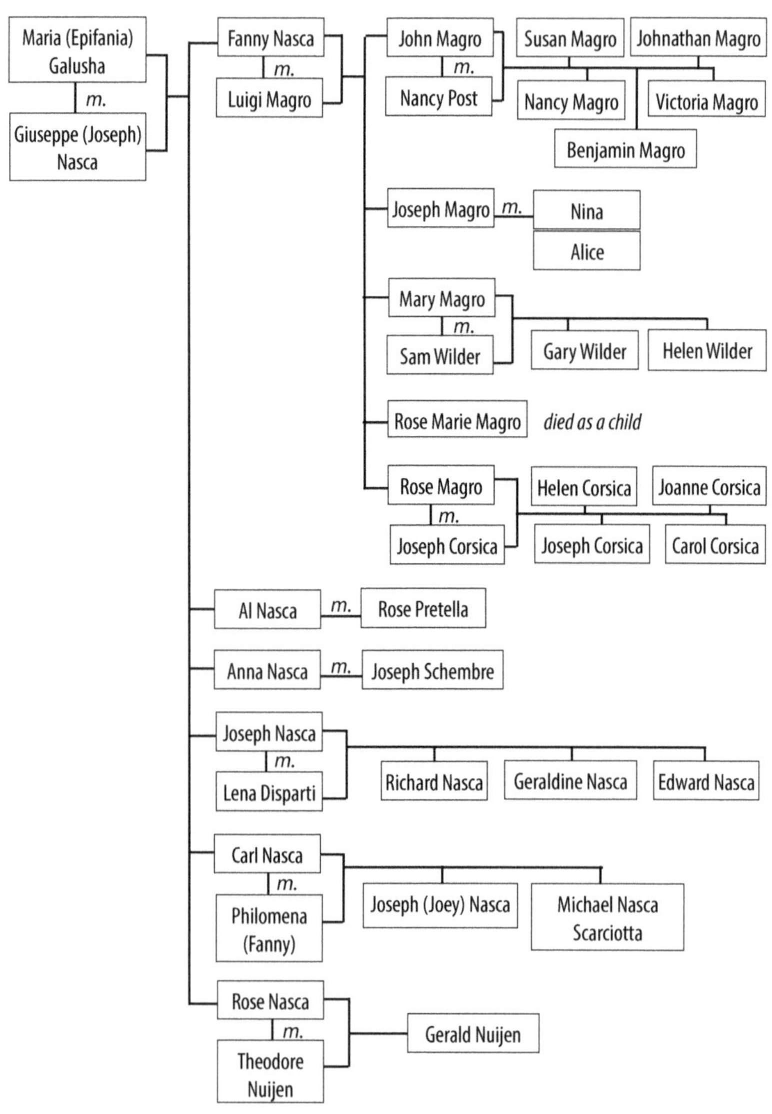

Nasca Family Tree

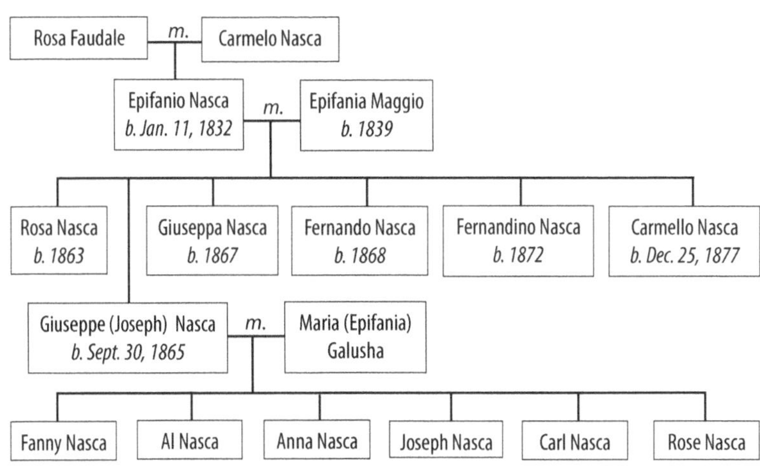

Dominic and Carnelia Galusha

Rosolino
Galusha
(changed
his name
to Russell
Williams) and
wife Rosena

Uncle Russell
at the wheel

Nunzio Galusha,
Josephine
Congelosi and
Antoinette
Galusha

Jimmy Galusha

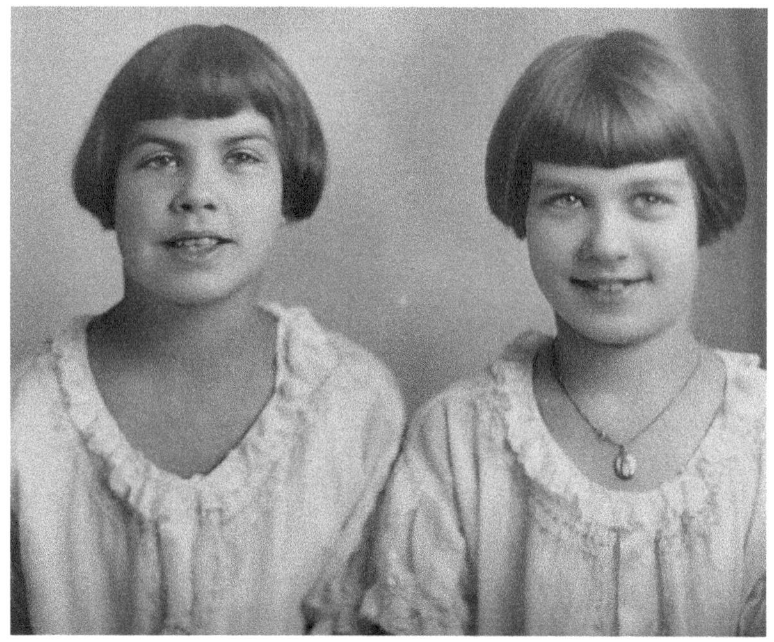

Anna and Dorothy Galusha, children of Jimmy and Lilian Galusha

Laurence, son of Frank Galusha

Loretta, daughter of Frank Galusha

Antoinette Congelosi, Lucy Galusha Congelosi, Josephine Congelosi Penna, Pascal Penna and Ignacio Congelosi

Pat Penna, Richard, Patty, Terry Penna, Ignacio Congelosi, George Kuchala, Annette Congelosi Kuchala, Lucy Congelosi and Josephine Pena

Castellan Sicily home of Ignacio Congelosi

Mary Magro, Rose Magro, Annette Congelosi, Rose Nuijen and
Josephine Congelosi

Terry, Pat, Josephine, Patty and Dick Penna

Maryanne and Dick Penna

Chris, Dick, Maryann, Rosemary and Suzanne Penna

Steven, David,
Frank and Patty
Laplaca

David, Nicole, Rosetta, Steven with little Victor. Seated: Meredith, Patty and Daniel Laplaca

PART III

CHAPTER 57

Joseph Nasca Meets Lena Disparti

Lena Louise was very outgoing and athletic. After completing her studies at the Geneseo Normal high school, she moved to Rochester, New York to obtain a business degree at the Darrow School. At Darrow, she learned to type, do bookkeeping and take shorthand. Lena worked as a bookkeeper for Torrey Jewelry for ten years. She lived with three roommates in Rochester and returned to Geneseo on the weekends to be with her family.

Lena Nasca age eighteen

Joseph A. was working with Kenneth Lily in the test room of the AT&T office in Rochester. Kenneth asked him if he would join him and his fiancé on a double date. After much pleading on Kenneth's part, he decided to go on the blind date. Lena had never been on a blind date and was somewhat reluctant to go, but was encouraged by her roommate, Ruthie Patterson, to give it a try.

Joseph A. Nasca

Lena and "Joe" found they had a lot in common, both being first-generation Americans with roots in Sicily. After a few dates, Lena brought Joe home to Geneseo to meet her parents and sisters.

At first, Nicolo was a bit concerned about the light-complected and smooth-talking Joseph A. However, he was a big hit with Fortunata and Lena's sisters. After a few visits and some conversation with his wife and daughters, Nicolo warmed up to his future son-in-law.

Lena was thirty-one and Joe was thirty when they got married on August 14, 1937, at St. Mary's Church in

Geneseo. Following the wedding, the reception was held at 37 Court Street. Joe had friends at Kodak who provided him with some of the first color film to make a movie of the reception. They honeymooned in Cape Cod.

Lena Disparti Nasca

Wedding party, August 14, 1937

A few months later, coming back from a party one evening, they were involved in a car accident which resulted in Lena Nasca suffering fractures of her upper and lower jaw. She had her mouth wired for several weeks. Later she lost several teeth and had to have dentures made.

A few months later, Joe was transferred to Elmira, New York, to work on the newly opened transmission lines between Elmira and Binghamton, New York. He had been in the Rochester AT&T office for ten years and was the second most senior employee. He was upset about his impending transfer. His appeals to stay in Rochester were turned down by management and he was sent to Elmira.

Joe and Lena moved to Elmira over Christmas of 1937 and lived in a rented duplex owned by the Robinsons. They made friends easily and enjoyed parties and social affairs with Joe's six coworkers in the Elmira AT&T office.

Rented duplex home, 1937 to 1941, Elmira, New York

On May 30, 1938, Richard was born at Arnot Ogden Hospital in Elmira. Papa Nasca came to live with them after Richard was born. The change of scenery and home environment lifted his spirits. He spent time with his new grandson and often did his diaper changes.

The doctors found a large venous blood clot in Papa Nasca's leg for which they had no treatment. One afternoon, Lena found him unresponsive sitting in the living room. He passed away in August 1939 from a pulmonary embolism.

Gravestones of grandparents Maria Epifania and Joseph Nasca

Richard was adopted by Charlotte Robinson, age six, who often took him out to make angels in the heavy snowfall and keep him entertained in the nearby playground.

Charlotte Robinson and Richard Nasca, age two, in Elmira, New York. 1940

CHAPTER 58

Move to Washington, DC

In 1941, at the start of World War II, Joe was asked to go to Washington, DC to work in the New York Avenue office of AT&T. He was recruited to work in K Carrier transmission. The New York Avenue office was the hub for all the government communications within the U.S. and to Europe. The coaxial cable system between New York and Washington was a vital link to the submerged cables from New York across the Atlantic to England and France. Joe and his coworkers worked twelve-hour days, seven days a week to keep these communications running during World War II.

Lena, Joe and Richard arrived in Washington the second week in December of 1941, by train from New York. AT&T provided them a room at the Hamilton Hotel in downtown Washington. Soon after they arrived, Joe went around town to see if a house was available to rent. When an owner found out that the Nascas had a three-year-old, they refused to rent the house to them.

The family spent Christmas at the Hamilton Hotel. The hotel had a beautiful Christmas tree in the lobby where little Richard would stop and ogle the bright lights and decorations on his way to the fine dining room. Although AT&T put no pressure on them to move out of the hotel, they badly wanted to find a home and resume a normal family life.

In early January, Joe was returning to work when he saw a sign in a window of a real estate company advertising an available row house for rent in the Anacostia section of Washington. Joe put a call in to the realtor who told him he would meet him at the house in an hour. Joe hailed a cab and went to 1409 18th Place, a few blocks south of the Anacostia River across the Sousa bridge. After inspecting the house, Joe told the realtor he wanted to rent it. After submitting his personal, financial and employment information, he got a call a week later from the realtor that he could rent the three-bedroom, two-story row house.

Frank Jeziseck, our next-door neighbor, was a bachelor and the bandmaster for the U.S. Navy Band. He became a surrogate father to Richard. He taught him to play the violin and work with his hands, and helped him plant his first vegetable garden in 1943 in his backyard. Our other next-door neighbor was Ernest Wartenberg, a navy chief with son Ernie and four girls. The neighborhood was full of young families, and Richard had a number of playmates at 18th Place.

CHAPTER 59

Move to Bethesda

In the spring of 1951, Lena read an ad in the Washington Post listing a home for sale in Bethesda, Maryland. She took a cab from Anacostia to Bethesda, a distance of fifteen miles, to see the house. She had decided to leave the rented house on 18th Place because the neighborhood was changing. White families were leaving and minorities were moving in. During the summer of 1950, there were riots a few blocks from our house in Fairlawn Park along the Anacostia River and several people were badly injured and a few were killed.

When Joe came home from work and had finished his dinner, she said, "I went to Bethesda today and saw a house I want to buy."

He turned to her and said, "Lena, you must be kidding. How are you going to be able to buy a house?"

She told him, "I have some money saved up that my parents gave me to use as a down payment on the house, and I plan to apply for a mortgage.

"The lady who owns the house is ill and wants to sell it. It is a three bedroom, one-and-a-half bathroom, brick Colonial on a half-acre lot with a large basement across the street from the Bethesda Naval Hospital."

That weekend, Joe reluctantly drove out to suburbia to see the Bethesda house. The town of Bethesda was small, with the tallest building the two-story Bank of Bethesda. There were a few grocery stores and shops, a movie theater, a drug store, a Hot Shoppes, a hardware store, a Catholic Church and grade school near the public high school.

When they arrived at the house, the owner was over-joyed to see Lena. Joe left the two ladies and went on a room-to-room inspection of the house. He quickly realized that the house would be an ideal choice for his young family, but he was very concerned about taking on a mortgage.

Lena told the owner, "Don't worry, I will buy your house, but it may take a little more time for me to get my husband to agree."

The owner said, "I have called my bank and told them I have a potential buyer and they are willing to talk with you and your husband about a mortgage."

A few minutes later, Lena and Joe were meeting with the owner's banker at the Bank of Bethesda. The bank could offer them a low-interest thirty-year loan. The monthly mortgage payment was a few dollars more a month that they were spending to rent the house on 18th Place. Joe finally caved in and agreed to sign for the mortgage.

A week later, Joe found out that a kitchen fire had occurred in the Bethesda house. The kitchen had been replaced and the owner had received insurance money for the damages. Based on the information about the undis-closed fire, Joe negotiated a lower sale price to which the owner agreed. Lena wrote a check for the down payment from her savings and the deal was closed.

In June of 1951, with the help of Sam Wilder and his

two brothers, we moved into our own home at 4700 Jones Bridge Road. I still remember Sam carrying our second refrigerator strapped on his back down 13 stairs to our basement.

After the excitement of the move was over and we were somewhat settled, I realized I had no friends. Mom suggested I dig up a plot along the back of the house to plant a garden. I put in six tomato plants, some peppers and cucumbers. I started mowing the lawn with a push mower, which took me a full morning. Before I realized it, I was back in school. The kids I met in my eighth-grade class at Our Lady of Lourdes accepted me and many of them became lifelong friends.

CHAPTER 60

Nasca Family in Bethesda

Moving from the city to the small town of Bethesda was a huge lifestyle change for our family. Dad had an hour's commute; Gerry and I had a longer walk to school at Our Lady of Lourdes and Mom had to do her shopping on the weekends when Dad was available to drive. The grocery stores were not within walking distance, as they had been in Anacostia, where Mom and I loaded groceries into my wagon for the walk home.

Mom got a job as a bookkeeper with the American Red Cross at the Bethesda Naval Hospital in 1958. The hospital was directly across the street from our house. She would walk across Jones Bridge Road, through a gate to her job. Later, she was picked up by neighbors who worked at the hospital. After a few months, she asked me to teach her to drive so she could carpool with her fellow workers.

Mom was very nervous behind the wheel, but she was a quick learner and mastered the clutch and standard shift on my 1950 Chevy in no time. Her major problem was parallel parking. For that, we spent time on the not-so-busy Wisconsin Ave., pulling into and out of parking spaces.

One day, Mom was driving my car to the store when she anxiously shouted out to me, "Richard, I see the road down near the brake pedal!"

I told her, "Nothing to worry about." I confirmed that

part of the floorboard had rusted out since she last drove the car.

That night she told Dad, "I think I am ready to purchase my own car."

A few days later, she and Dad found a blue four-door Ford automatic shift at a local car dealership on Wisconsin Avenue. Dad found that the automatic shift was mislabeled. When you placed the lever on "D" the car would go in reverse, and when placed on "R" it would go forward. The dealership refused to take the car back, so Mom learned to put the car in reverse if she wanted to move forward.

Dad retired from AT&T in March 1972 after more than forty-four years of service. Lena retired from the American Red Cross in 1971 after thirteen years and was the Secretary of the East Bethesda Citizens Association. They would go by Auto Train to Florida and spend winters in Dunedin, Florida. My future wife Carol's parents, Bill and Ida Smith, would join them for winter vacations while in Dunedin. They also traveled to Italy, Sicily, France, England, Spain and Hawaii.

CHAPTER 61

Richard Nasca

During my time in the sixth grade at St. Francis Xavier grade school in Anacostia, our Boy Scout leader left and our assistant resigned. Our troop was assigned to join the Boy Scout troop at St. Aloysius Church, a few blocks from the U.S. Capitol on North Capitol Street.

Our new Scout leader was Father Edward Fuller, a Jesuit priest who taught at Gonzaga, located behind the church. Our Saint Francis Xavier troop assimilated well with the troop of St. Al's. We went on several overnight and weekend camping trips riding in the back of an old army truck driven by Father Fuller. After our Scout meetings, we would do roller derby around the support posts in the basement under St Aloysius Church. During the summer of 1950, we spent two weeks at Camp Maria near Leonardtown, Maryland, fixing up the girls' camp. During that time, I learned to row a boat and paddle a canoe.

When it came time to choose a high school, Gonzaga was at the top of my list. Before I could apply, I had to pass the stringent entrance exam, and I did. I also took and passed the exam for the Priory Catholic High School, but decided that Gonzaga was a better fit for me.

I did well my first year at Gonzaga. However, my second year was marred by being late for class and having to spend many afternoons in JUG (Justice Under GOD).

Commuting from Bethesda to downtown DC consisted of taking buses, streetcars and hitching rides. One of my classmates, Vince Dougherty, had an old car and offered to pick me up at the Maryland /DC line. Vince was usually late and this resulted in both of us spending many afternoons in JUG.

I found it hard to put in the three hours of nighttime study and my grade point average started to decline, so by the end of the year, I was in the bottom quarter of my class.

During the summer between my second and third years, I decided that I needed a car to get to school on time. Dad bought me a gas-powered Jacobsen reel lawn mower, and I cut the neighbors' yards after delivering the morning edition of the Washington Post. I saved enough money to buy a rusted-out two-door, dark blue '50 Chevy stick shift.

My junior year at Gonzaga saw a turnaround in my grades, success in my quest to become a track star, and kudos from my classmates who encouraged me to change my ways and get back to being a good student.

During my senior year, I applied to the Georgetown College premed program but was accepted into the regular college program because of poor grades in science during my sophomore year at Gonzaga.

I did receive a half-scholarship to attend Georgetown since I had maintained an above-80 average during my four years at Gonzaga.

The plan was to do well the first year with the non-science courses and take Inorganic Chemistry during the summer after my freshman year. It just so happened that our neighbor, Dr. Wilson, was teaching Inorganic Chemistry that summer, and I did very well in his course.

I was transferred into the premed program of eighty students starting in my sophomore year. With the help of the guys in my study group, one of whom tape-recorded all the science lectures and had us over for dinner at his house once a week, the eight of us did well in the premed program and were all accepted into Georgetown School of Medicine class of 1964 which included 110 students.

I was fortunate to obtain a half-scholarship to the medical school, and since I lived at home, I was debt free. Mom was always there with hot meals late at night after my clerkships at the various hospitals. I was also fortunate to have access to the National Institutes of Health and the Bethesda Naval Hospital medical libraries plus other resources. Looking back at my career, matriculating at Gonzaga opened many doors to my future.

During my internship at the Hospital of the University of Pennsylvania, I met Carol Smith, RN, a chemotherapy nurse. We were married on April 16,1966 in the Cathedral Chapel in Philadelphia. Susan and Chris were born at Duke and Mark was born in Little Rock, Arkansas.

Chris, Carol, Dick, Susan and Mark Nasca

CHAPTER 62

Geraldine (Gerry) Seeber

Geraldine (Gerry) Nasca was born in Washington, DC, in 1943. At age two, she developed a staph ear infection that spread into the coverings of her brain, causing meningitis. Her pediatrician was able to obtain penicillin from Walter Reed Army Hospital. The penicillin (administered to the hospitalized soldiers and reconstituted from urine) saved her life.

After graduating from Our Lady of Lourdes grade school in Bethesda, Gerry went to Trinity High school in Georgetown. Richard drove Gerry to school since Trinity was only a few blocks from Georgetown College.

While at Trinity, she became friendly with Father Blakewell, a Jesuit priest who raised snakes and harvested their venom in the basement of Trinity Church, where John F. Kennedy and Jacqueline were married. She recalls that Father Blakewell had to move the snakes out of the church basement during President Kennedy's inauguration.

Gerry obtained her degree in Occupational Therapy from Richmond Professional Institute at William and Mary and practiced for sixty years in the Richmond area. She married Jim Seeber in 1967 and they had two daughters: Karen, who is a special education high school teacher, and Christine, who teaches Spanish at Roanoke College.

Gerry and Jim Seeber

Karen's graduation: seated, Karen and Christine; second row, Mrs. Nancy Seeber, Lena Nasca, Gerry Nasca Seeber; third row, Jim Seeber and Joe Nasca.

Christine, Jim, Karen and Gerry Seeber

CHAPTER 63

Edward Nasca

Edward Nasca was born in Washington, DC, in 1947. He graduated from Bethesda-Chevy Chase High School and received a bachelor's degree from Lambeth College in Jackson, Tennessee. He earned a master's degree in psychology at the University of Cincinnati and obtained a degree in hospital administration at University of Alabama, Birmingham.

Ed and Sheri retired to Black Mountain, North Carolina, and have two children, Liz and Mary Catherine.

Mary Catherine, Ed, Liz and Sheri Nasca

Gerry, Richard and Edward

CHAPTER 64
Leaving Bethesda

Nasca Bethesda Home at 4700 Jones Bridge Road

The Bethesda house was broken into during Easter 1980, while Lena and Joe were away. The robbers went through the entire house using candlelight, took all of Mom's wedding silverware, gold, and jewelry and Dad's watches. The robbers were subsequently apprehended. The police found a silver tray given to Mom on her retirement from the Red Cross in the home of one of the robbers. The silverware, gold, jewelry and watches had been sold.

The break-in greatly upset Mom, so she started looking around for another place to live. Dad wanted to stay in the Bethesda house. He was planning to get a dog and buy a gun. A neighbor, who was a builder, had offered him a low price for his house and he was reluctant to sell.

However, after the break-in, Mom said, "Joe, I have decided to move, with or without you."

Shortly thereafter, they moved to a large retirement community, Leisure World, in Silver Spring, Maryland. They lived in a spacious two-bedroom, two-bathroom first floor unit with a porch that opened up to a landscaped yard with well-cared-for grass, shrubs and trees.

In late 1987, Dad was treated for a low-grade bladder cancer. In spite of successful treatment, he continued to complain of lower abdominal discomfort. A barium enema was done, but the surgeon never called Dad in for a follow-up consultation. A few months later, he underwent surgery to remove a large cancer of the cecum and ascending colon which was causing severe obstruction. In addition, the cancer had already spread to his lymph nodes and liver. He did well after his first round of chemotherapy, but his response to the second round was not good, and it was decided to proceed with palliative care. Dad died at home in Leisure World in October 1989.

Lena continued to be active and in relatively good health until she fell during the night and broke her right hip in August 2000. A few days after the surgery to repair her hip, she went into renal failure.

During a return trip from Westminster, Maryland, in the fall of 1999, she turned to me as I was driving through the countryside lined with beautiful trees that were changing color and said, "Richard, I will not be here to see the leaves turn next year."

She died on September 28, 2000, the day the leaves started to turn from green to gold.

Lena Nasca's ninetieth birthday party. Mark Nasca, Karen Seeber, Christine Seeber, Lena Nasca, Chris Nasca, Mary Catherine Nasca, Susan Nasca and Liz Nasca.

Epilogue

After writing this story, I asked myself what motivated my grandfathers Disparti and Nasca to leave their homeland for the unknown. I decided that the "winds of change" that propelled them across the ocean were the desire for a better life for themselves and their families. Their hard work, willingness to take chances and acceptance of many significant challenges stand out. Also, sharing the fruits of their labor contributed to establishing the good life in America. Through their descendants, who now number in the hundreds, their legacy lives on in the daily lives of educators, social workers, therapist, physicians and others.

One can only wonder about our individual destinies if our ancestors had remained in Sicily.

Appendix

Latona

Antonio Latona, 1791 to 1871, and Agnes Guercio, 1793 to 1838, were the parents of Calogero Latona, my maternal great-grandfather born in Valledolmo, Sicily on June 24, 1837. Calogero's wife, Antonina Guinnuso, was born June 13, 1843. They were married in 1860 in the Church of Maria SS. della Pietra.

Calogero and Antonina had three children: Giovanni was born in 1862, Fortunata in 1874, Josephina (Giuseppa) in 1875.

Giovanni and his wife Louise had no children.

Fortunata and Nicolo had five children: Jerry, Genevieve, Lena, Caroline and Mary.

Jerry Disparti married Frances Giunta and had two boys, Nick and Carl.

Genevieve and Mary Disparti had no children.

Caroline died at age four.

Lena had three children with Joseph A. Nasca: Richard, Geraldine and Edward

Josephina and her husband, Charles Aprile, had six children: Carrie, Charles, Frank, Antonio, Marie Antoinette and Dominic.

Disparti

Salvatore Disparti married Antonina Lucania and had Girolamo Disparti, born in 1844. Nicolo Sangiorgio, born in 1828, married Concetta Saglimbene, whose daughter Vincenza, born in 1847, married my great-grandfather Girolamo Disparti.

Girolamo and Vincenza had Uncle Joe, Giuseppe Disparti, 1873 to 1951, and grandfather Nicolo Disparti, 1876 to 1959. After Vincenza died in 1896, Girolamo married Natalia De Marco. They had four children: Girolamo, Salvatore, Rosolino and Grazia.

Giuseppe Disparti married Caterina Toretta and they had a daughter, Vincenza, in 1889.

Disparti and Latona Family Tree

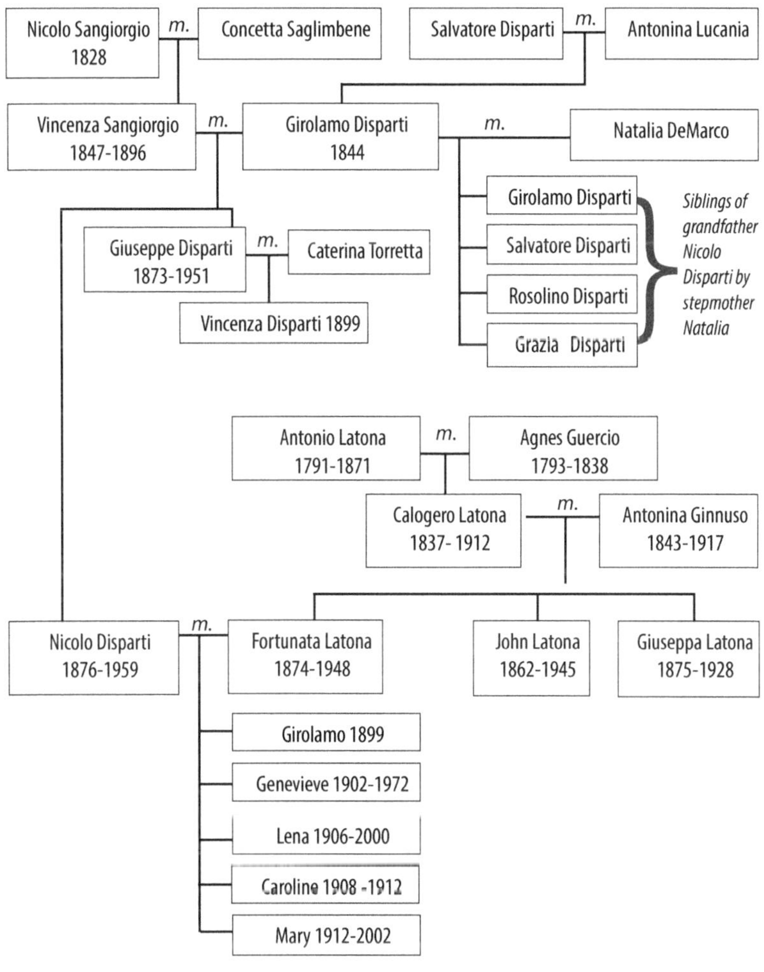

Galusha-Nasca-Magro Family Tree

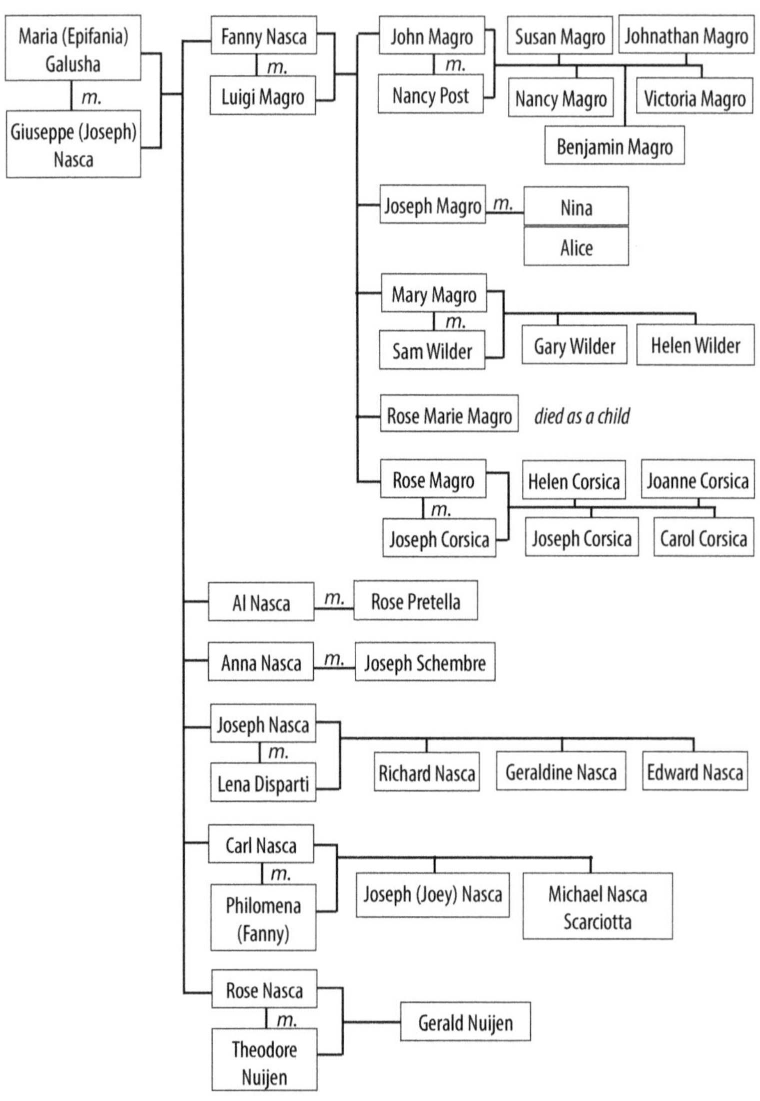

Galusha (Gugliuzza)

Loreto Gugliuzza and Antonina Ferraro had seven children: Frank, Lucy, Maria Epifania, Dominic, Jimmy, Rosolino (Russell) and Nunzio.

Frank Galusha and his wife Camella had two boys, Joseph and Sam. With his second wife, Mary, he had five children: Rose Amato, Josephine, Loretta, Rose and Larry.

Lucy Galusha married Ignacio Congelosi and had two daughters, Josephine and Annette.

Josephine married Pasquale (Pat) Penna and they had three children: Teresa, Richard and Patricia.

Annette married George Kuchala.

Dominic and his wife Carnelia had five children: Kitty, Larry, Rose May, Dominic and Josephine.

Jimmy married Lilian and they had two daughters, Anna and Dorothy.

Rosolino Galusha anglicized his name to Russell Williams and was married to Rosena.

Nunzio married Antionette and had no children.

Nasca Family Tree

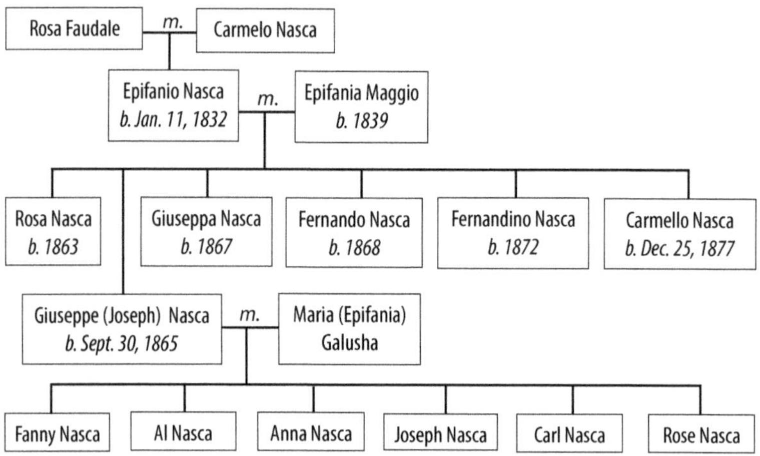

Nasca

Epifanio Nasca, born in 1832, was the son of Carmelo and Rosa Nasca.

Epifanio Nasca married Epifania Maggio, born in 1839. They had five children: grandfather Giuseppe Nasca, born in 1865, and Ferdinando, Fernando, Carmelo and Rosa.

Giuseppe (Joseph) Nasca and Maria Epifania Galusha had six children: Fanny, Al, Anna, Joseph, Carl, and Rose.

Fanny Nasca & Luigi Magro had five children: John, Joseph, Mary, Rose Marie and Rose Magro.

John Magro & Nancy Post had five children: Susan, Johnathan, Nancy, Victoria and Benjamin.

Joe Magro had no children with Nina or Alice.

Mary Magro & Sam Wilder had two children, Gary and Helen.

Rose Marie Magro died as a child.

Rose Magro and Joseph Corsica had four children, Helen, Joanne, Joseph, and Carol.

Al Nasca & Rose Pretella had no children.

Anna Nasca and Joseph Schrembre had no children.

Joseph A. Nasca and Lena Disparti had three children: Richard, Geraldine, and Edward.

Carl Nasca & Philomena (Fanny) DeFrancisco had Joseph (Joey) and Michael.

Rose Nasca & Theodore Nuijen had Gerald

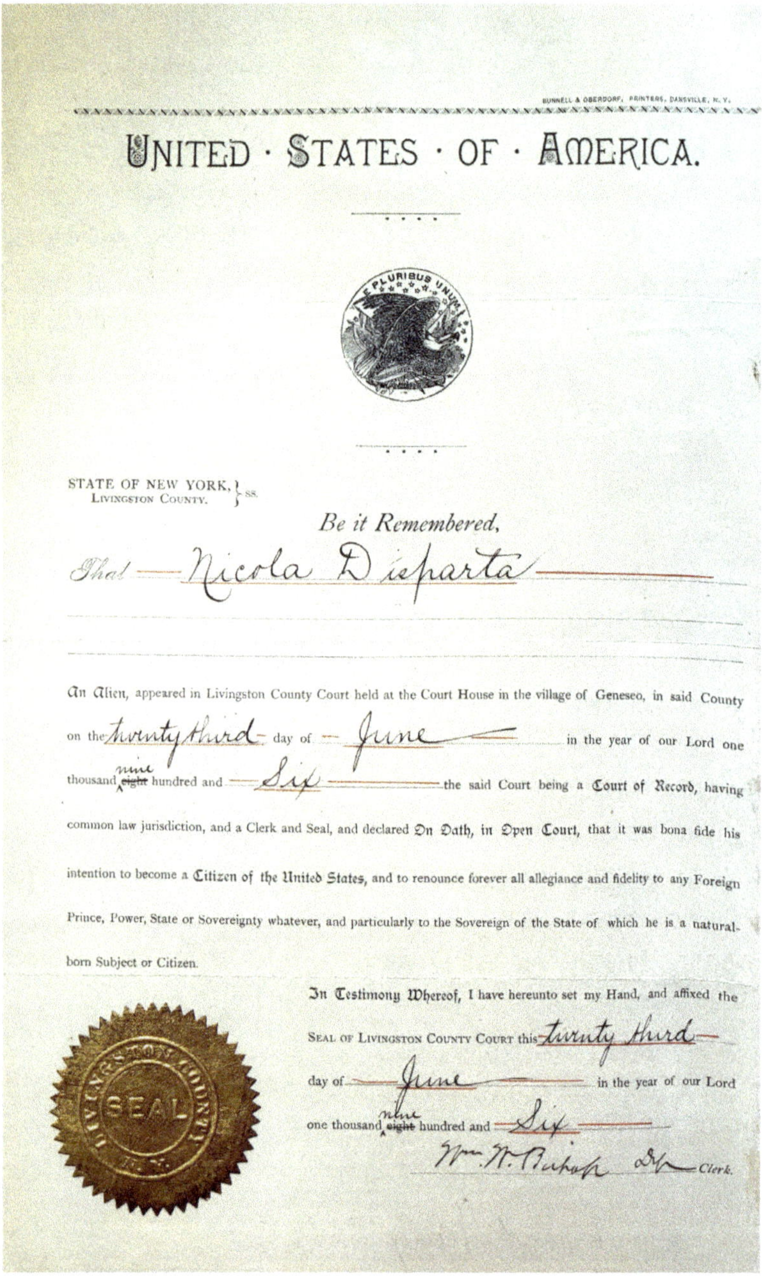

Nicolo Disparti Ccertificate of Naturalization, June 6, 1906

216

No. of certificate _139559_ 9

Name _Nicola Disparti_

Age, _35_ years

Declaration of intention issued by clerk of
County court of
Livingston County,
vol. _____, page _____, on the
_23_ day of _June_ A.D. _1906_
Petition filed on the _3_ day of _Jan'y_
A.D., _1911_, vol. _1_, page _37_
Name, age and place of residence of wife:
Fortunato Disparti,
_37_ _years,_
Geneseo, Livingston Co.
Names, ages and places of residence of minor
children: _Giloromo, 13 years,_
Vincenza, 8 years,
Antonina, 6 years,
Calogera, 4 years,
Fortunato 1 year, all
reside at Geneseo, Liv. Co.
Date of order: _June 26, 1911_
Vol. _1_, page _37_
Witness,
Wm Leonard _Nicola_ his X _Disparti_
(Signature of holder.)
mark

Screenshot of listing on Ancestory.com of my great-aunt, Giuseppa Latona, her spouse, and her father and mother, my maternal great grandparents.

Screenshot of listing on Ancestory.com of my grandmother Fortunata Latona and her parents.

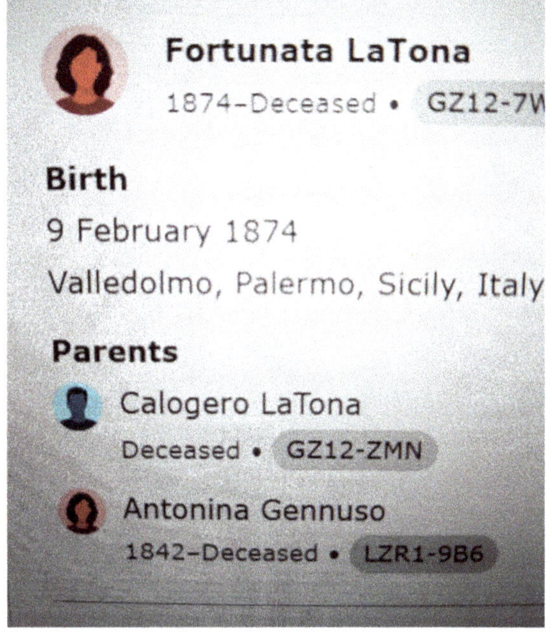

F43-2

BUNNELL & OBERDORF, PRINTERS, DANSVILLE, N.Y.

UNITED · STATES · OF · AMERICA.

STATE OF NEW YORK,
LIVINGSTON COUNTY. } ss.

Be it Remembered,

That Giovanni Latona

An Alien, appeared in Livingston County Court held at the Court House in the village of Geneseo, in said County on the 8th day of February in the year of our Lord one thousand eight hundred and two the said Court being a Court of Record, having common law jurisdiction, and a Clerk and Seal, and declared On Oath, in Open Court, that it was bona fide his intention to become a Citizen of the United States, and to renounce forever all allegiance and fidelity to any Foreign Prince, Power, State or Sovereignty whatever, and particularly to the Sovereign of the State of which he is a natural-born Subject or Citizen.

In Testimony Whereof, I have hereunto set my Hand, and affixed the SEAL OF LIVINGSTON COUNTY COURT this eighth day of February in the year of our Lord one thousand eight hundred and two

Wm H Clapp Dep Clerk.

First page of naturalization paper of Giovanni Latona

Alien—Minor. Petition, Affidavit, Etc.   U. S. Statutes at large, Vol. 32,
Chap. 1012, Sec. 39 and Chap. 927, Laws of New York, 1895.   A. R. Scott & Co., Book and Job Printers, Geneseo, N. Y.

County Court, County of Livingston.

In the matter of the Application of..
to be admitted to become a citizen of the United States of America.

To the County Court of the County of Livingston, State of New York:

The Petition of *Giovani Latona* .... of the town of ....County of Livingston, New York, respectfully shows:

That your petitioner was born on or about the........*17*........day of *May* ....
18*62*, in the..of....................................(State or Province.)
(County or Parish.)
....of....................................and
(Country)
that he immigrated to this country, and on or about the................day of ....
18*97*, arrived at the port of *New York* .... in the United States of America,
and that he bears no hereditary title and belongs to no order of nobility.

And your petitioner further shows that the grounds on which he claims the right to be naturalized are as follows:

A continuous residence within the limits and under the jurisdiction of the United States for five years and within the State of New York for one year or more, and a preliminary declaration of his intention to become a citizen of the United States, made before the County Court of the County of Livingston, State of New York, on the *8* day of *Feby* ...., 190*2*, a certified copy of which is hereto annexed and forms a part of this petition.

And your petitioner further shows, that his name in full is..
Giovani Latona ....that he was *42* .... years of age on his last birthday, and by occupation a .... and that he now resides at No.. Street, in the town of........................
County of Livingston, and State of New York, and that your petitioner intends to summon as witnesses at the final hearing upon his said application, ... residing at No.. Steect, in the town of........................
County of Livingston, and State of New York, and..
residing at No.. Street, in the town of........................
County of Livingston, and State of New York.

Your petitioner herewith presents, for filing herein, the affidavit of
Tony Aprile .... a citizen of the United States, as required by Sec. 3, Chap. 927, Laws of 1895, of the State of New York.

Wherefore. Your petitioner prays that all such process and proceedings may be had and taken herein as the law may require to enable him to become a citizen of the United States of America.

Dated *April 22* 190*2*

Giovanni Latona

Affidavit signed by Tony Aprile

Alien. Certificate of City or Town Clerk. Chap. 927, Laws of 1895.   **400**   Williamson Law Book Co., Publishers, Rochester, N. Y. 9-96

State of New York,

COUNTY OF *Livingston*

Village OF *Geneseo* } ss.

Town CLERK'S OFFICE.

I, *Chester C. Clark* Clerk of the said *Town* do hereby certify, pursuant to the provisions of Chapter 927, of the Laws of 1895, that *Giovanni Latona* has this day filed with me, as such Clerk, a notice in writing, stating that his full name is *Giovanni Latona*, age, *42* years, occupation, *Laborer* residence, No. , Street, in the *village* of *Geneseo*, County of *Livingston*, N. Y., and that on the *22* day of *April* 189*4* he filed his petition to be admitted to become a citizen of the United States, with the Clerk of the *County* Court, County of *Livingston*, and that the same is now pending therein.

In Witness Whereof, I have hereunto subscribed my name this *22nd* day of *April* 189*4*

Chester C. Clark

Clerk of the *Town* of *Geneseo*   N. Y.

Naturalization paper of Giovanni Latona, listed as a merchant.

Acknowledgements

I would like to thank Shelagh Clancy of Sea Leaf Book Editing for the many hours she spent in preparing the genealogy tables, the front and back covers, line editing, formatting the text and photos and uploading the manuscript for publication. Also, my thanks to my faithful and dedicated readers from the Landfall Writers' Group, Ed Hearn and Jack Bostrom, who did line by line editing. They and the other members of the Landfall Writers' Group continue to inspire me to write and have made valuable suggestions that enhanced the quality of the narrative, for which I am very grateful.

I appreciate Madeline Friedler, Livingston County Deputy Historian, for finding copies of Nicolo Disparti's and Giovanni Latona's naturalization papers and for sharing a great deal of information on the people who settled on Court Street in the early 1900s, contained in a booklet, "Court Street Community," published in 2012.

Special thanks to Shawn Mc Greevy who guided me through the genealogy research and to Trent Armbruster for her invaluable help on the final draft.

I very much appreciate the assistance of my sister, Geraldine Nasca Seeber, my brother, Edward Nasca, cousins Helen Wilder Gibson, Michael Scarciotta, Jerry Nuijen, Patricia Penna Laplaca, Richard Penna, Gerry Disparti, Joe Nasca, Susan Magro Pheil, Benjamin Magro,

Nancy Magro, Joanne Corsica, Chuck Aprile (deceased), Chip Aprile and David Laplaca.

Cover photo credits:

Ship: The SS Albania, completed about 1920 for Cunard, from a postcard on Flickr.

Palermo Harbor: Palermo Cala e Monte Pellegrino, by Giuseppe Incorpora (1834-1914), courtesy Wikipedia.

Ellis Island: Front facade of the Immigration Station at Ellis Island, photographer Edwin Levick, about 1913, courtesy Wikimedia Commons.

About the Author

Richard (Dick) Nasca is the grandson of Nicolo Disparti and Joseph Nasca. He is a retired Orthopaedic and Spine surgeon who lives in Wilmington, North Carolina. After a trip to Sicily with his sister, Geraldine Seeber, he decided to write a book about his grandfathers and their families.

Since he retired, he has written four children's books which are available on Amazon.com:

Paul Pro T is an illustrated story about the highs and lows of the game of golf as told by Paul Pro T, a golf ball. Written for children ages 5-10, the book includes a glossary of golf terms and tips on how to get started playing golf.

Tommy Tomato is an illustrated story that entertains and educates children ages 5-10 as they learn how to successfully grow a tomato. The book includes a helpful checklist and definitions of gardening terms.

Walter Watermelon is an illustrated story that is written to both entertain and educate children ages 4-8. The book includes helpful information about starting and maintaining a garden, as well as commonly used gardening terms, to encourage children to discover the joys of growing their own vegetables.

Billy Bluebird is an illustrated book about the life cycle of bluebirds Billy and Bonnie and their newly born offspring. The book is written for children 4-10 and contains information and instructions on how to build a bluebird house.

Dick has written five self-help books for seniors on orthopaedic conditions and their treatment with coauthor, James D Hundley M.D., an orthopaedic surgeon:

My Hip Hurts, My Knee Hurts, My Back Hurts, My Neck Hurts, My Shoulder and Elbow Hurt and soon to be published *My Wrist and Hand Hurt* are available on Amazon.com.

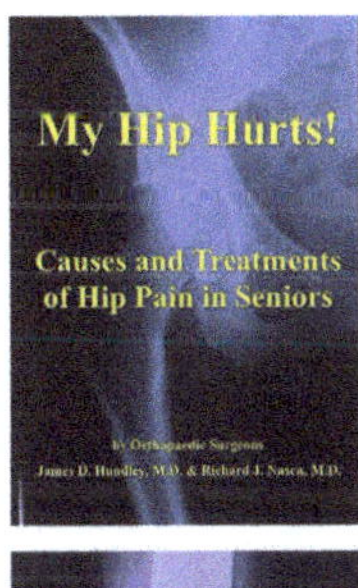

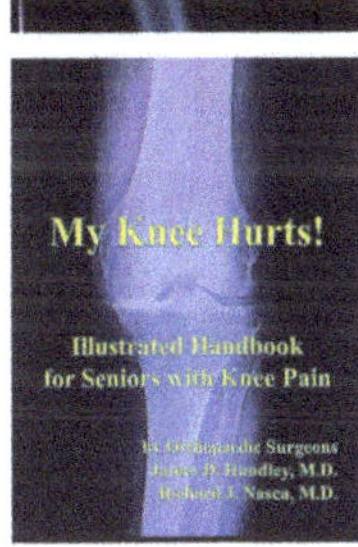

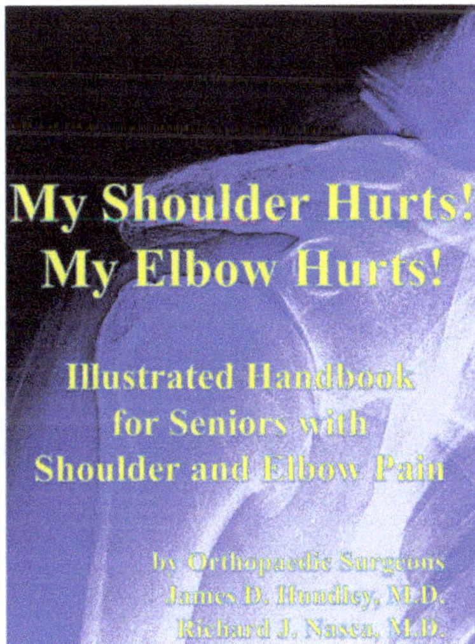

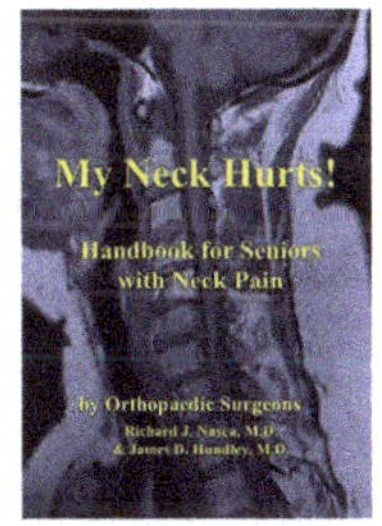

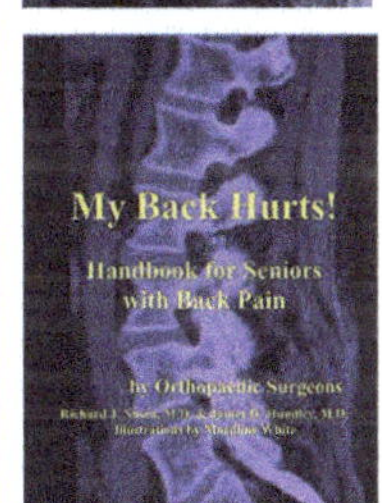

www.ingramcontent.com/pod-product-compliance
Lightning Source LLC
Chambersburg PA
CBHW041310120726
48005CB00014B/1948